**Higher Education in the Digital Age**

For Dick—
who is such a valuable
member of our team!

best~

Bill

11/19/14

# Higher Education in the Digital Age

**WILLIAM G. BOWEN**
*in collaboration with Kelly A. Lack*

with a new foreword by Kevin M. Guthrie

**ITHAKA**

*New York, Princeton, Ann Arbor*

**PRINCETON UNIVERSITY PRESS**

*Princeton and Oxford*

Third printing and first paperback printing, with a new foreword by Kevin
Guthrie and a new appendix by the author, 2014

Cloth ISBN 978-0-691-15930-0
Paper ISBN 978-0-691-16559-2

The Library of Congress has cataloged the cloth edition of this book as follows

Bowen, William G.
  Higher education in a digital age / William G. Bowen.
      p.    cm.
  Includes index.
  ISBN 978-0-691-15930-0 (hardcover : alk. paper)
    1. Education, Higher--Computer network resources. 2. Education, Higher--
  Effect of technological innovations on. 3. Internet in higher education. I.
  Title.
  LB2395.7.B67 2013
  378.1'7344678--dc23
                                      2013001913

British Library Cataloging-in-Publication Data is available

This book has been composed in Sabon, Gotham, and Scala Sans
by Princeton Editorial Associates Inc., Scottsdale, Arizona.

Printed on acid-free paper. ∞

Printed in the United States of America

10 9 8 7 6 5 4 3

*To Ezra,*
*my learned friend of many days,*
*and to the "Black Horse"*

# CONTENTS

# PREFACE AND ACKNOWLEDGMENTS

**WHEN PRESIDENT JOHN HENNESSY** invited me to give the
2012 Tanner Lectures at Stanford University, I accepted readily, in part because I had already been thinking for quite some
time about the twin subjects I would discuss: the "cost disease"
in higher education and the potential of technology (finally!) to
ameliorate the disorder. I spent much of the summer of 2012
pulling my thoughts together and working on drafts of the lectures, which were given in October of that year. Stanford
arranged to have the lectures complemented by formal commentaries from President Hennessy himself (who participated
actively in both the post-lecture discussions, as well as in the
two formal commentary sessions), Howard Gardner of Harvard University, Andrew Delbanco of Columbia University,
and Daphne Koller of Coursera.[1]

Peter J. Dougherty, director of Princeton University Press,
the long-time publisher of my books, expressed a strong interest in publishing a revised version of the lectures along with the
commentaries. We have now, in this book, the results of this
expression of interest.

The original lectures have been available on the ITHAKA
website since they were delivered, and printed copies have been

distributed to a number of people. The main part of this book consists of revised versions of the original lectures. In this preface, I will first describe what I have done—and not done—by way of revision. Second, I will acknowledge all that colleagues and friends did to help along the way. But I want to anticipate the acknowledgments by emphasizing at the outset of the preface that Kelly A. Lack, a colleague at ITHAKA for the last two and a half years, has been my active collaborator in both the initial preparation of these materials and then the revisions.[2] I regard her as a full partner in this enterprise even though I cannot pass off on her, or on anyone else, my full responsibility for the final content.

In thinking about the revisions that I would like to make, I first decided that I would keep the informal, conversational character of the lectures. Next, I decided against introducing new topics. That would have delayed publication and worked against my desire to maintain a certain tone and tempo. There are, to be sure, important follow-on research projects, which I reference in the text of this book, but they will have to be addressed in due course and stand on their own. I also decided that I would do my best to incorporate new developments that appeared after the lectures and that were related to the existing lecture content. This has been a daunting task for Kelly and for me, but a stimulating one. We have learned new things. We did have to set an end date, however, and we decided that we would try to limit our inclusion of developments that occurred after Thanksgiving 2012. And we recognize that we have, inevitably, missed some materials published before our end date. This is such an incredibly "active" field that there is no way two mortals could claim to control all of it on a "real time" basis.

One other stylistic matter. In the main, I have kept—and added to—the copious endnotes, now exceeding 150 in total, that were an integral part of the text that appeared on the ITHAKA website right after the lectures. These endnotes report the sources of opinions and other materials cited in the text; they also provide additional commentary that would have overwhelmed the text had I put it there. Some readers may find the endnotes more useful than the text, and in a few cases (but only a very few) I have moved original endnote material to the text. Readers who either heard the lectures or read online versions of them may want to know the main changes in this revised text. The structure remains the same. The book is in two parts, which track quite closely the objectives of the two lectures. Part 1, which contains the revised version of the first Tanner Lecture (henceforth referred to as Tanner I), sets the context by discussing the "cost disease" and related trends, the productivity concept as it applies to higher education, affordability, and whether rising educational costs deserve to be regarded as a real crisis. Part 2, which contains the revised version of the second Tanner Lecture (henceforth referred to as Tanner II), explores the multiple challenges we confront in trying to use technology, and variants of online learning in particular, to provide at least something of a "fix" for the cost disease. Below I summarize the revisions I have made to each lecture.

Tanner I. In addition to updating references, I have included:

- comments by President Hennessy on recent trends in the published tuition rate and student aid at Stanford, which has had the ability (and will) to increase student aid faster than tuition—a pattern that stands in stark contrast to what has happened at many (less wealthy) institutions, both private and public;
- a more nuanced discussion of the components of the productivity ratio that emphasizes the importance of both reducing institutional costs (the denominator of the ratio) and improving student-learning outcomes such as completion rates and time-to-degree (in the numerator); it also

recognizes that there is a "consumption" component on the output side of college education;

- a suggestion that publications stop making unsupported blanket condemnations of higher education as inefficient;
- a list of additional factors pushing up college costs (such as the increased expenses associated with benefits, including the effects of higher Medicaid charges in some states);
- a softening of the assertion in the original version of Tanner I that improving the match between student qualifications and the standards of the institutions they attend would improve overall completion rates;
- an even stronger emphasis on the need for new research into the "revealed preferences" of students as they make enrollment decisions in response to escalating tuition charges in the public sector;
- a brief reference to the November 2012 vote in California to permit higher taxes in lieu of further sharp reductions in state support for education; these taxes have been seen by some as resuscitating hopes for more generous state support (though I do not agree with this optimistic assessment); and
- an even stronger warning that if colleges and universities themselves do not address the cost and affordability issues that beset public higher education, elected state officials may seek to impose strong incentives for educational institutions to meet what could be overly narrow, short-term state objectives.

Tanner II. The quite extraordinary—and seemingly unremitting—surge in discussions of online learning, and especially of massive open online courses (MOOCs), has encouraged us to make a number of revisions to the discussion of the potential of technology to address the issues highlighted in the first lecture. Here are the additions:

- an explicit recognition of our lack of any real understanding of teaching effectiveness in conventional classroom settings, as well as when online learning is used;
- an emphasis on the likelihood that improvements in pedagogy, and greater experience in using online learning, will almost certainly lead to better learning outcomes over time than the ones we reported in ITHAKA's May 2012 empirical study of the effectiveness of the Carnegie Mellon statistics course at public universities—we now regard those results as setting a kind of baseline;
- recognition that the greatest potential for MOOCs to improve productivity probably lies in their creating more flexible scheduling opportunities, easier ways of gaining transfer credits, and a general re-engineering of the entire educational process in some settings;
- references to recent progress in addressing certification issues, including the minimization of cheating, that enhance the likelihood that MOOCs can raise completion rates and lower time-to-degree for the system as a whole;
- a clearer recognition that no one platform or tool kit is likely to become dominant, and of the value of competition among a variety of platforms provided by both not-for-profit and for-profit entities;
- discussion of experimentation by developers of MOOCs in finding sustainable sources of revenue (e.g., by charging fees to institutions like Antioch University that plan to use MOOCs in their credit-granting curricula); and
- consideration of the potential of technology to permit unbundling of some functions performed by faculty, thereby moving us some distance from a vertical to a horizontal educational model—with profound implications for decision-making and the role of faculty in governance (which are key topics in need of serious study).

## Acknowledgments

As I have already said, Kelly A. Lack has been my chief collaborator in all aspects of this study. I cannot thank Kelly enough for her highly effective work and, beyond that, for her endless patience with me and her friendship. She has a great future ahead of her. I suspect that, right now, Kelly is more familiar with the burgeoning literature on online learning than anyone in the world!

Among the many others who have contributed ideas and have commented on early drafts, I want to single out three people:

- Lawrence S. Bacow, former chancellor of the Massachusetts Institute of Technology and former president of Tufts University, who is now "president-in-residence" at the Harvard Graduate School of Education;
- Kevin M. Guthrie, president of ITHAKA; and
- Michael S. McPherson, president of the Spencer Foundation.

These three have been indefatigable in making incisive comments, clarifying points, and offering non-stop encouragement. All three will be engaged in follow-on studies sponsored, at least in part, by ITHAKA.

Others who have offered valuable comments include:

- William J. Baumol, now professor at NYU's Stern School of Business and the academic director of Stern's Berkley Center for Entrepreneurship and Innovation;
- Paul Benacerraf, professor of philosophy emeritus at Princeton University;
- Henry S. Bienen, president emeritus of Northwestern University and chairman of the ITHAKA board;
- Derek Bok, president emeritus of Harvard University;

- Laura Brown, managing director of JSTOR and executive vice president of ITHAKA;
- William E. ("Brit") Kirwan, chancellor of the University System of Maryland;
- Daphne Koller, co-founder of Coursera;
- Deanna Marcum, managing director of the consulting and research arm of ITHAKA, Ithaka S+R (which stands for strategy and research);
- W. Taylor Reveley III, president of the College of William and Mary;
- James Shulman, president of ARTstor;
- Robert Solow, institute professor, emeritus; professor of economics, emeritus, MIT;
- Richard R. Spies, formerly executive vice president for planning and senior adviser to the president, Brown University; and
- Sarah E. Turner, professor of economics and education at the University of Virginia.

Colleagues on the staff of ITHAKA who have worked on key parts of this research agenda include Matthew M. Chingos, now at the Brookings Institution; Thomas I. Nygren, now a lecturer in the Centre for English Language Studies at Sunway University in Malaysia; and Ithaka S+R staff members Rebecca Griffiths and Matthew Staiger. Susanne Pichler, librarian at the Andrew W. Mellon Foundation, has been of great help in finding references and suggesting places to look for additional material. I am sure my colleagues would agree that my long-suffering wife, Mary Ellen Bowen, should be regarded as an informal member of the team. She has offered, as always, much good advice and, in addition, has been my "techie" out of the office.

Johanna Brownell, my executive and research assistant, has been extraordinary in the way that she has overseen this entire process, from composition to revision to publication, and has taken responsibility for locating obscure materials, making numerous improvements in the exposition, and putting the final manuscript in good order for publication.

The funders of the pieces of related research that are the backbone of these lectures are the Carnegie Corporation of New York, the Bill & Melinda Gates Foundation, the William and Flora Hewlett Foundation, the Stavros Niarchos Foundation, the Spencer Foundation, and an anonymous foundation. In addition, the Andrew W. Mellon Foundation has generously supported key infrastructure costs. Those of us who have worked on this set of studies are grateful for the support provided by all of these funders—we could not have managed without it.

The contributions of the commentators at Stanford on these lectures have already been noted. I learned a great deal from all of them.

This research is an integral part of ITHAKA's program. I want to thank ITHAKA, led by the chairman of its board, Henry S. Bienen, and its president, Kevin M. Guthrie, for steady support and encouragement.

Finally, I want to thank my friend Peter J. Dougherty, director of Princeton University Press, and Seth Ditchik, executive editor for economics and finance, who has had direct responsibility for overseeing the publication of this book. No author could ever ask for stronger, or more professionally adept, support from a publisher.

*November 22, 2012*

## Notes

1. Coursera is a social entrepreneurship company that offers online courses to the general public, currently free of charge.
2. ITHAKA is a nonprofit organization whose mission is to help the academic community use technology to advance research and teaching in sustainable ways.

# FOREWORD TO THE PAPERBACK EDITION

WHEN THE MANUSCRIPT FOR the hardcopy edition of this book went to press, it was Thanksgiving 2012. The world was rapt with what *The New York Times* had called "The Year of the MOOC." A number of widely known commentators were predicting that disruption was rapidly to come to higher education, mainly based on comparisons to what had happened in other industries. Things have not changed as rapidly as predicted and many now want to proclaim that MOOCs are irrelevant. But *Higher Education in a Digital Age* was not, and is not, a book tapping into the hype surrounding MOOCs. It is a thoughtful and data-rich evaluation of the economic and political forces that are challenging higher education, and the technological and cultural developments that may provide a way to address them. It continues to be as relevant in today's fast-moving environment as it was when it was first published, even as Bill Bowen, and those of us who work with him at ITHAKA, continue to conduct research to understand better both the impact and the potential of these developments.

In the time between the publication of the original hardcover and this paperback edition, Bill Bowen has written two papers providing additional commentary on the issues raised in this book. One of them, the written version of the Stafford

Little Lecture given at Princeton University in October 2013, is included in its entirety in as an appendix to this paperback. The other paper, published in *EDUCAUSE Review* on October 2, 2013, is available on the EDUCAUSE web site.[1] Both comment on—and speculate about—where these developments are taking us and what barriers exist to making faster progress in using technology to improve educational outcomes without commensurate increases in cost.

In this foreword, I want to provide a brief overview of Ithaka S+R's current research agenda, which builds on both this book and the two recent essays just mentioned. We believe this research agenda outlines the major questions facing higher education in the coming years. We expect that these projects will lead to further publications.

In brief, Ithaka S+R is embarked on a coordinated series of studies led by ITHAKA staff and its senior advisors, working in collaboration in many instances with Michael McPherson and his colleagues at the Spencer Foundation. The projects listed below, underway now and at various stages of development, are all designed to provide valuable evidence and analysis that will help higher education leaders address the challenges ahead.

## The National Context

Our starting point is the proposition that this country's system of higher education needs urgently to address two inter-related issues:

1. The need for more (and better-educated) human capital if the U.S. is to be competitive in an increasingly knowledge-intensive world; and

2. Widespread concerns about the capacity of the country's educational system to foster social mobility at a time of increasing inequality in resources and in opportunities (see President Obama's statements on inequality and, for

example, the editorial in the *New York Times* endorsing Obama's comments).[2]

The two concerns interact because it is highly unlikely that the U.S. can increase markedly its stock of human capital without broadening the reach of higher education so that more students receive a high quality education that will prepare them for satisfying and productive lives. Of course, concerns about inequality and the need for social mobility in a society that has prided itself on "opportunity" are also directly relevant. To address these concerns will require our colleges and universities to continue to raise college completion rates and to reduce time-to-degree—for both students overall and for students from lower socioeconomic status ("SES") families. Achieving these results while managing costs and maintaining quality will be essential if our higher education institutions are to slow increases in tuition and control net costs facing students and their families.

As many have pointed out, there have been substantial cutbacks in public support for higher education in recent years, impacting both four-year and two-year institutions. It seems clear that substantial increases in public support, however desirable or even justifiable, are unlikely to be forthcoming, given fiscal and political constraints. That prospect, and the limited ability of families to afford further tuition increases, has an obvious implication: there will be ever-more emphatic calls for improvements in "productivity"—in output per unit of input. Higher education, writ large, simply has to reengineer its processes to find more cost effective ways to meet students' education needs.

It is not enough to bewail the shortcomings of the present system of higher education. Nor is it enough simply to exhort colleges and universities to do better. To find possible solutions it is essential that we understand the roots of the problems with the current system and identify the obstacles to overcoming them. That is where we think rigorous research can play a valuable role.

**Ongoing Ithaka S+R projects**

- *Maryland Studies of the Effectiveness of Modified MOOCs and Other Online Systems*: Working closely with Chancellor William (Brit) Kirwan, colleagues at the University System of Maryland, and faculty from a number of Maryland campuses, our staff have conducted a series of case studies and side-by-side tests to compare the learning outcomes of traditionally taught on-campus courses with those taught using MOOCs and two adaptive online learning platforms (one based on Coursera offerings and one based on Pearson products). These studies shed light not only on how students' learning outcomes and experience are impacted by these new platforms, but also provide insight into the practical challenges of using externally generated content and learning platforms to support instruction in particular institutional contexts.[3]
- *The Evolution of Faculty Roles in Governance*: For reasons explained in detail in this book and in the other two essays cited earlier, we have come to believe that it is important to understand how faculty roles in governance have evolved over the years within different types of educational institutions. It is by no means obvious that inherited structures of "shared governance" are well suited to ensure that colleges and universities can (1) take full advantage of faculty capacities to contribute constructively in the exploration of new uses of online technologies; and (2) address needs to innovate across established organizational lines, recognizing, for example, that issues of scale and cost argue against every campus or department developing its own solutions at its

own pace. We are combining a broad historical overview with a number of case studies designed to highlight different governance approaches at different types of institutions (including public universities, private colleges, and private universities.)

- *Protocols for Defining IP Rights*: This study focuses specifically on what is still largely uncharted territory—namely, how colleges and universities are recognizing and distributing "ownership rights" to new offerings, whether they be individual courses or platforms, including how to oversee distribution of new materials. More thought needs to be given to how to address complex issues of "sustainability" (for example, how users of new offerings, including users on campuses other than the "home campus," can be sure that the offerings will continue to exist and even to be improved over time).

- *Evolving Staffing Patterns*: Staffing patterns, including the growing use of adjuncts and professional teachers, also deserve careful attention. There is a strong case for thinking freshly, as some are now doing, about how non tenure-track faculty are to be employed—what their roles should be, what opportunities for advancement should be offered, and how their increasingly important presence should affect governance arrangements.

- *Potential Cost Savings*: The potential impact of these new technologies on costs deserves more thought (and rigorous analysis) than it has received. We are interested in exploring both what can be learned from recent experiments with various teaching methods and what educational gains and cost savings might be obtained from fresh uses of new forms of online learning. Because the creation of new courses and platforms incurs additional cost initially, and many potential savings are not fungible and cannot be realized immediately, we are working to develop simulations that model a future state where some of the existing institutional constraints are relaxed. One question of particular interest is how greater flexibility in scheduling might encourage both higher completion rates and some reduction in time to degree.

- *Implications of New Patterns of State Support for Public Higher Education*: We are interested specifically in the implications of these new patterns for both access and educational success, especially for "near-poor" students who are not eligible for Pell grants but who nonetheless face serious financial challenges as tuition goes up. We are focusing on experiences to date in the public university system in Virginia.

- *Public University Collaborations in Developing and Using Technology*: With financial support from the Lumina Foundation, Ithaka S+R has conducted nearly 250 interviews at ten public research universities to assess the potential for these institutions to collaborate in developing and using technology. Interviews have been conducted with departmental chairs, faculty, and administrative officers in an effort to understand the needs, benefits, and challenges related to technologically-enhanced collaborations. We expect the report on these interviews will yield insights beyond the potential for collaboration to include such topics as governance, barriers to implementation of new technologies, and the impact of budget structures on incentives and outcomes, among others.

- *Update of Summary of Online Research Findings*: Ithaka S+R staff are updating the summary review of research findings about studies in online learning. (The original study, by Kelly Lack, is included in this book.)

This list of projects provides an outline of our view of the major issues that face leaders of higher education institutions today. What is going to be the impact of MOOCs and new adaptive learning platforms on learning outcomes? Will these save resources or increase costs? Will governance structures need to be adapted to enable the kinds of innovation required to meet rapidly evolving needs of students and society? How will IP rights in the new learning materials and platforms be managed and maintained over time? And how will the balance between research and teaching be struck in the future? We believe that the thoughtful reflections in this book have lasting value in helping both leaders of colleges and universities, and others actively involved in setting policies, frame these and other issues in ways that are appropriate in their specific settings. The over-riding goal is to help higher education use technology to achieve outcomes that are both better and more cost effective.

Kevin M. Guthrie

September 2014

## Notes to the Foreword to the Paperback Edition

1. See http://www.educause.edu/ero/article/potential-online-learning-promises-and-pitfalls.

2. See *Remarks by the President on Economic Mobility*, the White House, December 4, 2013. Also see "The President on Inequality," the Editorial Board of the *New York Times*, December 4, 2013. Also relevant is New York Mayor Bill de Blasio's "Tale of Two Cities" theme and other commentaries on inequality in the U.S.

3. See http://www.sr.ithaka.org/research-publications/interactive-online-learning-on-campus.

# CONTRIBUTORS

**William G. Bowen** is president emeritus of the Andrew W. Mellon Foundation and Princeton University.

**Andrew Delbanco** is Mendelson Family Chair of American Studies and Julian Clarence Levi Professor in the Humanities at Columbia University.

**Howard Gardner** is the John H. and Elisabeth A. Hobbs Professor of Cognition and Education at Harvard University and senior director of Harvard Project Zero.

**John L. Hennessy** is the president of Stanford University.

**Daphne Koller** is the Rajeev Motwani Professor of Computer Science at Stanford University and cofounder of Coursera.

# Part 1

## Costs and Productivity in Higher Education

AS MY WIFE keeps reminding me, I have a Don Quixote–like tendency to flail away at windmills—to take on topics such as race in America and affirmative action; the insidious problems with college sports at all levels, including Division III and the Ivy League (which cause me to cringe whenever the NCAA refers to its legions of "student-athletes"); and, yes, the unforgiving economics of labor-intensive industries, such as the performing arts and higher education. But, my DNA is what it is, and so I am now adding to this list the potential implications of online learning for college costs.

Context matters, and I will begin by outlining as succinctly as I can aspects of the economics of higher education that are relevant to my topic:

- trends in costs, the "cost disease," and how to think about changes in productivity;
- other forces, some deeply ingrained in the fabric of higher education, that also push up costs; and
- growing worries about affordability, especially in the public sector, where reductions in public support have been coupled with significant increases in tuition.

Then, in the second part of the book, I will discuss what I think—or, better said, what I *suspect*—about the potential impact of the variety of approaches to online learning that are everywhere present, including, of course, at Stanford University and at Stanford spin-offs such as Coursera and Udacity. Is there, as President Hennessy has suggested, a tsunami of some still ill-defined kind coming? Is it realistic to imagine that online learning is a "fix" (at least in part) for the cost disease? Throughout, I will maintain a system-wide perspective, since it will not do to think about these large questions solely from the perspective of individual institutions.

### Cost Trends, the "Cost Disease," and Productivity in Higher Education

It is fitting that I gave these Tanner Lectures in close proximity to Clark Kerr's neighborhood, since it was President Kerr, in his capacity as chairman of the Carnegie Commission on the Future of Higher Education, who commissioned a study of mine in the mid-1960s that became *The Economics of the Major Private Universities*. In that study I documented the seemingly inexorable tendency for institutional cost per student (which is, of course, different from tuition charges) to rise faster than costs in general over the long term. Kerr christened this finding Bowen's Law, although he was, he said, "originally skeptical about it."[1]

What is important today is not the exact numbers contained in that study (which were based largely on a detailed examination of the experiences of the University of Chicago, Princeton University, and Vanderbilt University between 1905 and 1966) but the underlying pattern, which has been found to hold for public as well as private universities, and for colleges too. I reproduce here, as something of a historical relic, a figure from my 1960s Carnegie study (figure 1). The figure shows that,

**Figure 1** Direct costs per student, compared with an economy-wide cost index

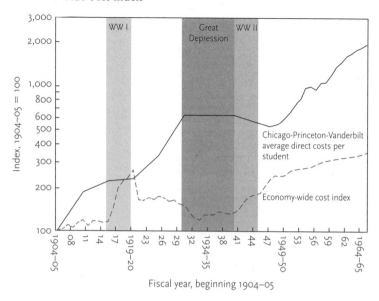

excepting war periods and the Great Depression, which require separate analysis, cost per student rose appreciably faster than an economy-wide index of costs in general. The consistency of this pattern suggested to me then, as it does today, that we are observing the effects of relationships that are deeply embedded in the economic order.

Running through all the factors at play (and there are many, as I will indicate shortly) is a key proposition that my teacher and lifelong friend, William J. Baumol, and I first articulated in our study of the performing arts, which also dates from the mid-1960s.[2] The proposition is known to this day in the literature as the "cost disease." The basic idea is simple: in labor-intensive industries such as the performing arts and education, there is less opportunity than in other sectors to increase productivity by, for example, substituting capital for labor. Yet markets dictate that, over time, wages for comparably qualified individuals have to increase at roughly the same rate in all industries. As a result, unit labor costs must be expected to rise faster in the performing arts and education than in the economy overall.

Robert Frank of Cornell University provided this succinct explanation of the cost disease as recently as March 2012: "While productivity gains have made it possible to assemble cars with only a tiny fraction of the labor that was once required, it still takes four musicians nine minutes to perform Beethoven's String Quartet No. 4 in C minor, just as it did in the 19th century."[3] In short, productivity gains are unlikely to offset wage increases to anything like the same extent in the arts or education as in manufacturing; hence, differential rates of increase in costs are to be expected—a finding Baumol and I reported for major orchestras at about the same time that my Carnegie study of higher education was under way.[4]

About a decade after the Carnegie study, I reported a similar pattern in my 1976 President's Report at Princeton: "While prices in general have risen about 50% [over the previous 10 years alone], the most widely used price index for higher education has risen about 70%."[5] And in 2012, three and a half decades later, Sandy Baum, Charles Kurose, and Michael S. McPherson reported basically the same pattern. In their paper "An Overview of Higher Education," presented at Princeton University, they cite a careful study using data from the Delta Cost Project that shows that "educational expenditures per FTE student increased at an average annual rate of about 1% beyond inflation at *all* types of public institutions from 2002 to 2008."[6] There is no need to burden this argument with more data about trends in institutional costs, which are notoriously hard to interpret, in part because they often involve aggregations of various kinds. It is easy to get mired in the underbrush, and we do well to remember the admonition of the architect Robert Venturi: "Don't let de-tails wag the dog."

There is, however, a final big point to note about trends—namely, the reversal that has occurred in the last decade or so in the respective positions of private and public institutions. When I wrote my 1976 report, from the perspective of the president of a private university, there was widespread concern about the widening gap in charges between the privates and the publics (with the privates becoming ever more expensive relative to the publics). In those years, the privates were hit especially hard by the stagflation of the time, with its dampening effect on stock market values that, in turn, affected both returns on endowments and private giving. Today, it is the publics that have suffered more than most of the privates (and certainly more than the most selective privates), largely as a result of sharp cutbacks in state appropriations.

During a discussion session the day after I originally made these remarks at Stanford, President Hennessy contrasted trends in tuition and student aid in the public sector with the recent experience at Stanford. He observed that while Stanford's "sticker price" has continued to increase, as it has throughout almost all of higher education, Stanford has had the financial wherewithal to increase its outlays on student aid by even more than the increases in its tuition and has chosen to spend some part of its resources in this highly commendable way. Only a small number of other wealthy private institutions have been able to do the same thing, and the fortunate circumstances of these relatively well-off "outlier" institutions should not be allowed to obscure the general pattern pertinent to the public colleges and universities that educate three-quarters of this country's college students[7]—or, for that matter, the trends pertinent to the large number of private colleges and universities that have also been compelled to raise tuition faster than they have been able to raise student aid. I will return in due course to the broad subject of increasing stratification in higher education and its implications.

I am aware that thus far I have been using an important word—*productivity*—without defining it. Put simply, productivity is the ratio of outputs to the inputs used to produce them. But this formulation conceals at least as much as it reveals, since it is maddeningly difficult in the field of education to measure both outputs and inputs—even within a single institution, never mind across institutions serving different missions. If only we produced standardized widgets or harvested blueberries!

As one illustration of how treacherous this terrain is, the National Academy of Sciences released, in 2012, a massive report of over two hundred pages devoted to the measurement of productivity in higher education. A major virtue of the report, which in turn cites a voluminous literature, is that it debunks the idea that productivity in higher education is unidimensional. It warns against a multiplicity of dangers that lurk behind the use and misuse of (inevitably) simplified measures. The report insists that "quality should always be a core part of productivity conversations, even when it cannot be fully captured by the metrics."[8] It also emphasizes the complications stemming from joint production of outputs such as teaching and research, and the need to recognize a complex mix of inputs, including capital and student time.

In thinking about the implications of these myriad complications for the ways in which technology might impact the cost disease, I have been helped greatly by the authors of an article in the *New England Journal of Medicine* (*NEJM*), who have captured quite skillfully factors that explain what is known as the IT productivity paradox—the apparent tendency, noted by Robert Solow of MIT in 1987, for computerization to fail to improve standard measures of productivity. Solow noted famously, "You can see the computer age everywhere but in the productivity statistics," an observation said to have launched more than two decades of research into the sources of the paradox.[9]

The authors of the *NEJM* article argue that explanations for the IT productivity paradox fall into various categories. Under the heading of "mismeasurement," they note that "important dimensions of service output such as accessibility and convenience—factors that are greatly improved by IT—are difficult to quantify and are rarely captured by productivity metrics."[10] For example, ATMs increased consumer convenience in banking, but this increase in convenience, and all the time saved by customers, was not captured by traditional measures of productivity.

The authors go on to point out: "In terms of 'mismanagement,' the introduction of new technologies usually forces reexamination of the assumptions that underpin less productive processes." They give a telling example concerning the introduction of electricity in manufacturing: early on, "factories simply swapped large electronic motors for waterwheels and steam engines but retained inefficient belt-and-pulley systems to transmit power from the central power source. Real productivity gains came only after manufacturers realized that many small motors distributed throughout a factory could generate power where and when it was needed."[11]

This discussion in the *NEJM*, aimed at implications for the health industry, resonates with the uses of IT in education. It is easy to think of examples, including the tendency in the early days of online teaching simply to mimic typical classroom teaching methods, often by videotaping lectures, rather than re-engineering the teaching process as a whole.

From the standpoint of our interest in the cost disease, it is critical to keep in mind that *the productivity ratio has both a numerator and a denominator.* Productivity improvements can be either output-enhancing (raising the numerator) or input-conserving (lowering the denominator). It seems evident that information technology has been extremely consequential in higher education over the last twenty-five years, but principally in output-enhancing ways that do not show up in the usual measures of either productivity or cost per student. It is important to distinguish between at least two broad types of educational "output": research findings and student learning outcomes. We should also recognize that there is a consumption component in the output numerator. The veritable revolution in information technology has had an especially large impact on research output. Data management systems and powerful number-crunching capacities have permitted research that would have been simply impossible otherwise. Work in particle physics and studies of the human genome are but two examples from the physical and life sciences. To cite a much more mundane example from the social sciences, the work that Derek Bok and I did on the effects of race-sensitive admissions would have been impossible without the construction of the large College and Beyond database.[12] More generally, advances in communications, and the development of networks and systems for managing text and exchanging perspectives with colleagues at a distance, have revolutionized the way papers are prepared and revised—again and again! Yet these innovations do not show up at all in the usual measures of output.

Technology has also led to dramatic improvements in the scholarly infrastructure. If I may again cite activities that I know well, the creation of JSTOR (a highly searchable electronic database of scholarly literature) has changed fundamentally the way scholars use the back issues of journals and has had profound effects on libraries. Similarly, ARTstor (a digital repository of high-quality images) now permits art historians to study, for example, images of a Bodhisattva on the wall of a cave in Dunhuang, an oasis town on the Silk Road, alongside images of the same Bodhisattva on a silk painting at the Guimet Museum in Paris.[13] It is worth emphasizing that these benefits generally do not accrue to the institutions that made the investments necessary to realize them. For example, the extraordinary time savings for scholars made possible by both JSTOR and ARTstor do not prompt the institutions that employ the scholars to harvest these savings by, for example, increasing teaching loads (unimaginable!).

Although faculty and students have certainly benefited in many ways from easy Internet access, relatively little has happened with respect to classroom teaching—until quite recently. In the second part of this book, I will suggest that we are only at the beginning of the kind of re-engineering that could in time transform important parts—but only parts—of how we teach and how students learn. Most fundamentally, I will argue that we need to improve productivity in two ways: (1) through determined efforts to reduce costs—that is, we need to focus more energy on lowering the denominator of the productivity ratio; and (2) through new ways of increasing the student-learning component of the numerator of the ratio, principally by raising completion rates and lowering time-to-degree.

## Factors Other Than the Cost Disease Pushing Up Educational Costs

As important as I believe the cost disease to have been (and to be) in putting upward pressure on instructional costs, I certainly do not think that it is the sole villain. Let me now mention ever so briefly three other forces behind the rise in costs. I recognize, of course, that this list is by no means comprehensive.[14]

### Inefficiencies

I am not one of those who looks with disdain at how poorly managed colleges and universities are often alleged to be. (I have seen too much of other organizations in all sectors of the economy, including the for-profit sector.) It is at least mildly annoying when, with no attempt to provide evidence, a business publication such as *Forbes* blithely asserts on its cover (of November 19, 2012) that "no field operates more inefficiently than education."[15] I wonder if that is really true. Perhaps the time has come—if it is not past—when we should cease making such sweeping pronouncements (recognizing that colleges and universities in general have had much greater staying power than many for-profit businesses, which have been seen to fall by the wayside in surprisingly large numbers).

Still, it is hardly surprising that the severe financial pressures of our time have led to renewed calls for more business-like approaches. One consulting firm, Bain & Company, has found that universities such as the University of California, Berkeley, the University of North Carolina, Chapel Hill, and Cornell University are complex, decentralized institutions that could save money by simplifying oversight structures and centralizing functions such as human resources, information technology, and purchasing.[16] In my view, just as it is wrong for business-oriented writers to assert that inefficiency is rampant, it is also unwise for academics to dismiss studies such as these out of hand as contributing to a "corporate mindset" in higher education. Universities do have to become more business-like in relevant respects at the same time that they have to retain their basic commitments to academic values.

I would, however, caution against too facile an acceptance of the assumption that when universities devote increasing shares of their resources to non-instructional infrastructure costs, they are demonstrating inefficiency. That may or may not be true. In some instances, regulatory requirements compel universities to spend more on compliance. There are also situations in which it makes excellent business sense to substitute lower-cost inputs for faculty time spent on mundane tasks that others can do at least as well. Of course, none of this is to deny that wasteful "bureaucratic creep" can occur.[17]

It is also true that educational institutions are good at adding things but not good at subtraction. Fixed costs are often truly fixed (such as the costs associated with cutting-edge scientific laboratories in narrowly defined fields). Moreover, universities are collections of highly specialized talents that cannot be readily shifted from, say, teaching Russian to teaching Spanish. Institutional rigidities are facts of life that in many, though hardly all, cases derive from the very nature of the academic enterprise. It is harder, however, to defend antiquated organizational structures such as "centers" of one kind or another, which are notoriously difficult to dismantle even when they have ceased serving their purposes. A good rule of the road is to use flexible structures such as workshops or experimental colleges that do not take on lives of their own.[18]

Still more controversial aspects of alleged inefficiencies on the academic side of the house are the scope of program offerings, the use of cross-subsidization to support low-enrollment programs, and the reluctance to use differential tuition pricing to ration costly offerings and encourage students to go into less costly areas. The value propositions at issue are vigorously contested, and I can do no more here than recognize the importance of this debate.[19]

### An Ingrained Desire to "Buy the Best"

Institutional proclivities are a powerful factor of a very different kind. Charles Clotfelter, in his detailed case studies of costs at elite universities, found that there was a determination to spend whatever it took to excel.[20] There is, indeed, a deep-seated commitment to enhancing institutional reputation. Given this mindset, the availability of resources is a strong driver of costs.[21] Lawrence S. Bacow, former chancellor of the Massachusetts Institute of Technology (and former president of Tufts), has said that at MIT, "the mentality was to do what we needed to do to make sure our students mastered the material, regardless of cost. . . . We looked to reduce class size, increase teacher-student contact, do more hands on learning, etc. All of these drive costs up and productivity down."[22] Moreover, faculty and students often collaborate to create inefficiencies. An example is Friday classes, which neither students nor faculty want; it is very difficult for presidents to prevent the demise of these classes when students and faculty agree on such an objective.

Competitive juices are everywhere evident, and I confess that I am conflicted in how I feel about this undeniable source of upward pressure on costs. In company with other economists, I believe that competition to "be the best" drives up quality and is basically a good thing. The competitive (entrepreneurial) nature of American higher education stands in sharp contrast to what one often finds elsewhere and is, I believe, a key reason why many American research universities are the best in the world. In recent years, however, I have come to wonder whether, in some situations, there can be too much competition for the societal good. We have seen more and more stratification within higher education, with the wealthiest institutions distancing themselves from other very good, but not so wealthy, places.[23] I believe this combination of increased stratification and a determination to buy the best can have some pernicious effects. For instance, wealthy institutions routinely make huge investments in the start-up costs of faculty hires in the sciences. This puts great pressure on other places that think of themselves as peers to match such outlays, even if they have to divert funds from needy fields such as the humanities.

I worry, too, that the financial aid policies of wealthy institutions apply too much de facto pressure on other institutions to be extremely generous, thereby encouraging "quasi-merit-aid-wars" of dubious societal value. Students and their families complicate all of this by applying pressure of their own for more and more amenities (elaborate student centers and fitness facilities, dormitories that sometimes have features that 99 percent of the population can't enjoy, and so on). Institutions feel that they have to satisfy the desires of full-paying affluent families who (not surprisingly) want more and more of everything, including customization.[24] This is hardly surprising in a society in which it is now possible to order highly customized clothing by clicking online. But, of course, the multiplication of choices is expensive. Still another complicating (I would say "aggravating") factor is the *U.S. News* rankings, which encourage institutions to put too much weight on maximizing their yields and keeping up their average SAT scores even as more and more evidence casts doubt on the predictive value of these scores.[25]

There is a conundrum here. Institutions have an understandable interest in always improving themselves, even if the pursuit of immediate institutional self-interest cuts against larger societal interests. Still, the most privileged places should think hard about the ramifications of their actions. When I spoke at the installation of Morton O. Schapiro as president of Williams College, I used a quotation from the Midrash Tanhuma: "The rich should ever bear in mind that his wealth may merely have been deposited with him to be a steward over it, or to test what use he will make of his possessions."[26]

There *is* a stewardship responsibility. Moreover, American colleges and universities are so fiercely competitive that consideration has to be given to benign forms of collusion and even some regulation. Reluctant as I am even to mention the NCAA in any kind of quasi-favorable light, we should acknowledge that there is value in obligatory academic requirements (minimal as they are) for participation in intercollegiate sports.[27] I also think that some years ago the U.S.

Department of Justice did us all a disservice in applying simplistic notions of antitrust regulation to well-designed efforts to ensure that limited financial aid resources were in fact distributed on the basis of agreed notions of financial need.

As another example, President Bacow has suggested that universities might consider limiting tenure to some number of years. The objective would be to combat the costly and sometimes corrosive effects of the end to mandatory retirement.[28] I should confess that when I was a beginning graduate student I was one of those who objected to mandatory retirement, which was legal at the time. I was in the last class that the brilliant economist Jacob Viner ever taught at Princeton on the history of economic thought. Summoning up all my courage, I went into Professor Viner's office to complain about his impending retirement. Viner gave me one of his most piercing looks and said, with a twinkle in his eye: "Mr. Bowen, most of what you say is true. I am at the peak of my powers, smarter than all of my colleagues, and it would be a shame if future Princeton students were deprived of the opportunity to learn from me. But," he added, "your conclusion is wrong. I should be forced to retire. I'll tell you why. My colleagues are good and compassionate people, and they will never distinguish me from all of the other faculty members who should have retired years ago! Either all of us go, or none of us goes. It is much better that all of us go." Here is the end of the story: Professor Viner did have to retire from Princeton, but he went on to teach at leading universities all over the world until his death.

There is a place for well-considered rules, especially when they allow markets to work (as in Viner's case). More generally, I believe that there is a need for a thoughtful study of situations in which some collusion is a good thing, as well as situations in which collusion is injurious.

Back to the implications of the relentless pursuit of reputation. One specific problem—a definite source of upward pressure on costs that I attribute in no small degree to status wars—is the proliferation and at times excessive support of graduate programs of middling status in fields such as physics. Neil Rudenstine and I discussed this problem at length in a book we wrote some years ago (*In Pursuit of the PhD*), and there is no evidence that it has done anything but become more serious since.[29]

Robert M. Berdahl, when he was president of the Association of American Universities (AAU), courageously asked: "How many research universities does the nation require? . . . I do not know how many we should have. But it is a serious question, worthy of examination."[30] Berdahl's probing question led to a two-year, congressionally mandated assessment of financial threats to the nation's research universities. The study did not, however, answer Berdahl's central question—which is, to be sure, highly sensitive. William ("Brit") Kirwan, chancellor of the University System of Maryland, has called this a missed opportunity "to address that very point more explicitly."[31] I agree.

During my time at the Andrew W. Mellon Foundation, I tried a slightly different tactic—namely, to encourage, with the carrot of substantial grant funding, some universities with PhD programs that were not highly ranked to substitute less expensive yet stronger postdoctoral programs for them. I was dismayed to find that many presidents agreed privately with my assessment of what made sense but were unwilling to take the political heat that would have been generated by an effort to dismantle any PhD programs. Worries by faculty about potential loss of status in the profession overwhelmed all else, and presidents who had other battles to fight were unwilling to risk struggling with faculty on this issue, with all of its symbolic overtones.[32]

Less controversial and every bit as fundamental are two systemic issues: (1) ineffective supply-side provision of higher education by some institutions, combined with weak incentives for students to finish programs in a timely way; and (2) what is known as the mismatching problem.

Sarah Turner and colleagues, in an important and underappreciated paper, have documented a marked increase in time-to-degree (TTD) over the last three decades.[33] If it takes longer for students to complete their degrees, and if large numbers never finish, the implications for productivity are clear. As someone observed, "The most expensive degrees are those that are never obtained"—or, one might add, the ones that require five, six, or more years to obtain.[34] A lengthening of time-to-degree could, of course, be the result of an influx of poorly prepared students, but Turner and her colleagues have demonstrated rigorously that this is not the main source of the problem. Indeed, they found that "the increase in TTD is localized among those who begin their postsecondary education at public colleges outside the most selective institutions." A combination of declines in resources at these less selective public institutions and the tendency for students to work more hours for pay (at the expense of finishing their studies) is at the root of the problem.

There is abundant evidence that undergraduate students who fail to graduate in four or four and a half years often take more credits than they need, in part because of inadequate guidance, starting and stopping majors, and a lack of places in gateway courses.[35] Student attitudes are another part of the problem. A recent graduate of a highly selective flagship university in our *Crossing the Finish Line* study said that at his university, graduating in four years was like "leaving the party at 10:30 P.M."[36] But we are starting to see reports that schools are now addressing the problem of long TTD more aggressively, by altering the way they charge for credits and pushing "super-seniors" to graduate in a timely way. There is less willingness to tolerate five- or six-year graduation rates.[37] Easing transfer paths from two-year to four-year institutions would also make a considerable difference, and places like the City University of New York are making active efforts to facilitate flow through the system.[38]

There is also strong evidence that both lower completion rates and longer time-to-degree are caused in no small measure by the failure of surprisingly large numbers of well-qualified students to enroll at colleges and universities for which they are qualified, ending up instead either at less challenging institutions or at no postsecondary institution at all. The primary source of this problem is at the application stage: large numbers of students, and especially students from poor families and some minority groups, simply do not apply to institutions at which students with their qualifications do well. The University of Chicago Consortium on Chicago School Research played a pivotal role in introducing into this discussion the concept of "match"—that is, the match between the student's qualifications and the selectivity level of the college he or she actually attends. The Chicago Consortium has described in detail the frustrating experience in its city of watching students who had worked hard and successfully in high school then fail to take advantage of the potential college-going opportunities that they had earned. In *Crossing the Finish Line,* our research team found strong evidence of this same "undermatching" phenomenon in North Carolina.[39]

The serious consequences of this persistent pattern are related directly to the by now well-documented empirical relationship between completion rates and the selectivity of colleges and universities. Even after controlling carefully for differences in the observable qualifications of entering students, evidence shows that students who attend institutions that enroll high-achieving students are themselves more likely to graduate, and to graduate in four years, than are comparable students who attend less selective institutions. This finding may seem counterintuitive at first—shouldn't it be easier to graduate from less selective (and presumably less rigorous) schools than from those that are more selective and more rigorous? But the finding is correct. Presumably peer effects, differences in expectations for graduation, opportunities to work closely with faculty, and institutional resources such as libraries and laboratories are very important.[40]

Two major research projects are now under way to study alternative ways of alleviating the mismatch problem: one is directed by the research organization MDRC in New York, and one is led by Professors Caroline Hoxby from Stanford University and Sarah Turner from the University of Virginia.[41] Success on this front would reduce disparities in outcomes related to socioeconomic status by raising timely completion rates for well-qualified students, often from disadvantaged backgrounds, who currently mismatch. It is also possible that improvements in match would raise overall completion rates somewhat, though this is conjectural and there is no hard evidence of which I am aware. Much depends on the elasticity of the supply of places at moderately selective institutions and on what would happen as a result of any reshuffling of the student population that would occur because of better matching.[42]

## Affordability

The word *affordability* has achieved iconic status; it became a part of the ad wars in the 2012 presidential campaign. Is higher education affordable today for students and their families? Will it be affordable tomorrow? These are key questions to ponder, but they do not lend themselves to simple answers.

This is a murky terrain, and I hope you will be pleased to know that I intend to ride roughshod over it.[43] For my purposes, it will suffice to note commonly cited numbers generated by others and emphasize a limited number of basic points.

At the root of much of the discussion of affordability is the well-known fact that state appropriations per student have declined sharply in recent years, both in absolute terms and relative to other sources of revenue.[44] According to one study, the state appropriations share of the total receipts of public colleges and universities fell from 44 percent in 1980 to 22 percent in 2009.[45]

Particularly in recent years, the price students pay for college at public universities has risen faster than per-student costs (never mind prices in general)—at the same time that these universities have experienced reductions in state and local support.[46] Public systems seeking to avoid cutbacks in enrollment and to maintain quality have had little choice but to raise charges. A 2012 College Board report states: "Over the 30 years from 1982–83 to 2012–13, the increase for in-state students [in average published tuition and fees] at public four-year institutions was 257%, from $2,423 to $8,655";[47] furthermore, "the growth in published prices at public four-year institutions has been higher over the past decade (averaging 5.2% per year beyond inflation) than over either of the two preceding decades."[48] Net charges have increased less rapidly because of both efforts to augment financial aid and the substitution of some federal dollars, including stimulus aid, for state dollars. Still, *net* tuition as a percent of total educational revenue in public higher education rose from 23 percent in 1986 to 43 percent in 2011 (figure 2).[49]

Furthermore, as Joseph Stiglitz, the 2001 Nobel laureate in economics and former chief economist of the World Bank, has emphasized: "Parents' ability to pay without resorting to debt is declining. . . . The income of the typical American family, adjusted for inflation, declined from 2007 to 2010. Their wealth

**Figure 2** Net tuition as a percentage of total educational revenue in U.S. public higher education, fiscal 1986–2011

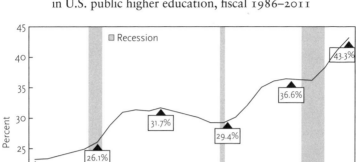

*Note:* In calculating these figures, net tuition revenue used for capital debt service is included in net tuition but excluded from total educational revenue. Years are state fiscal years, which commonly start July 1 and run through June 30 of the following calendar year. For example, FY 1986 is July 1985 through June 1986.

*Source:* State Higher Education Executive Officers, SHEF—State Higher Education Finance FY 2011, 2012, http://www.sheeo.org/resources/publications/shef-%E2%80%94 -state-higher-education-finance-fy11.

was down almost 40%. Separate data show that household income is back to the levels of a decade and a half ago."[50] Economic conditions have indeed taken a toll, and those who complain that college costs are rising faster than incomes should recognize that stagnation of median family incomes is definitely one blade of this scissors.

It is important to recognize that these trends do not appear to have led most students and their parents to conclude that college is not for them or is simply beyond their reach. Indeed, 83 percent of college students and parents participating in the most recent Sallie Mae/Ipsos survey strongly agreed that "education is an investment in the future,"[51] and a majority

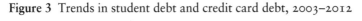

**Figure 3** Trends in student debt and credit card debt, 2003–2012

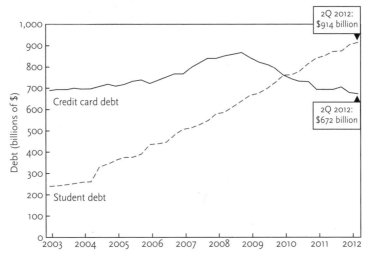

*Source:* Federal Reserve Bank of New York, "Household Debt and Credit Report," September 30, 2012, http://data.newyorkfed.org/householdcredit/.

said they were "willing to stretch [themselves] financially" to make this education possible.[52] Strong demand for higher education appears to be ever present, but it would be helpful to have more hard evidence than is available now as to the actual effects on student behavior of increases in tuition and changes in financial aid policies at public universities.[53] It would be a mistake to assume that the apparent lack of big effects to date guarantees that there will be no adverse effects in the future.

We get closer to the core of affordability concerns when we recognize that the combination of upward trends in charges and deteriorating family circumstances has led to a large increase in student debt—which, as has been widely reported, now exceeds credit card debt (figure 3).[54] For many students, borrowing has become the only option. Student debt has risen sharply—though nothing like as astronomically as the incredibly inept story in the Sunday *New York Times* of May 13, 2012 suggested.[55] The *Times* originally reported that 94 percent of bachelor's graduates leave college with educational debt. The correct number is around two-thirds, as Sandy Baum and Michael S. McPherson pointed out in their devastating commentary on the *Times* article.[56] An equally troubling aspect of the *Times* article (again quoting Baum and McPherson) is that it "focused on a student who has more debt than almost every other college graduate and who chose to enroll at an institution, Ohio Northern University, where average debt levels exceed those at almost every other college in the country."[57] As a colleague of mine now at the Brookings Institution, Matthew M. Chingos, wryly observed: "Share of student borrowers with >$54k debt: 10%; share of grads interviewed by *NYT* with >$54k debt: 100%."[58] Gross misreporting and fear-mongering do not encourage thoughtful consideration of a complex issue.

Professors Christopher Avery and Sarah Turner have made a commendable effort to create an analytical framework that can be used to think through borrowing decisions.[59] They ask whether (and when) college students borrow too much, *and* whether (and when) college students borrow too little. Much depends, they explain, on the aptitudes/talents of an individual, choice of major, institution attended, likelihood of actually getting a degree, career interests and prospects, and so on. An important conclusion of their research is: "The claim that student borrowing is 'too high' across the board can—with the possible exception of for-profit colleges—clearly be rejected."[60] There are many cases in which students elect (often unwisely, I believe) not to borrow modest sums needed to finish degree programs in a timely way, choosing instead to work so many hours on off-campus jobs that they either delay completing their programs or do not complete them at all.[61] U.S. Department of Education data show that most students have been graduating with what seem like manageable debt loads. According to data from the Department of Education, three-quarters of four-year graduates owe less than $33,857 on earning a degree—often much less.[62] The Pew Research Center recently reported that the average outstanding student loan balance was $26,682 in 2010 among all households with student debt; the Pew study also shows (not surprisingly) that the *relative* burden of student debt is greatest for households in the bottom fifth of the income distribution.[63]

In correcting overwrought worries about student debt, I do not want to go to the other extreme. Many students surely borrow too much and have their lives affected adversely. There is evidence that high debt may make students less likely to choose lower-paying jobs which might well prove more satisfying, and this is one reason why I favor combining loan programs with forgiveness features that take account of job choices.[64] An irony is that many students attending highly selective, wealthy universities such as Princeton and Harvard should be the best candidates to borrow at least modest sums to pay part of the costs of their education—yet these are the very institutions that, for what are surely praiseworthy reasons, have elected to adopt grant-only financial aid programs. As I suggested earlier, an unfortunate consequence is that less wealthy colleges and universities can feel pressured to adopt financial aid policies that are unwise for them.

Reluctance to take on even a modest amount of debt may also have a sizeable impact on college choice and contribute to the mismatch problem described earlier. Where one goes to school is by no means the be-all and end-all, but it can be important. I am reminded of an experience I had in the aftermath of the publication of the book Derek Bok and I wrote on affirmative action.[65] I was at a gathering in Washington, DC, when a white woman stood up and said that surely there are many fine schools in America, and she couldn't understand why minorities made such a fuss about getting into a place like Stanford. An African-American woman stood up and replied: "Wait a minute. Are you telling me that all those white folks fighting so hard to get *their* kids into Stanford are just ignorant? Or are we supposed to believe that attending a top-ranked school is important for the children of the privileged but shouldn't matter to minorities?" There was dead silence. Interestingly, the evidence we presented in *The Shape of the River* shows that the gains associated with attending the most selective schools are, if anything, greater for minorities than for whites.[66]

### Is There a Serious Problem—Even a Crisis?

There are certainly reasons to think so. Among measures of educational outcomes, more and more attention is being focused on completion rates.[67] Yet, in spite of President Obama's exhortations,[68] various Department of Education initiatives, and vigorous efforts by the Gates and Lumina Foundations, among other private players, there is no evidence that levels of educational attainment in the United States are rising to match the progress made in other countries.[69] Moreover, serious questions have been raised regarding the capacity of America's higher education system to deliver on a second core mission: to enhance mobility and serve as a powerful equalizer—as an engine of opportunity. Scholars have found evidence that achievement gaps between rich and poor children have been increasing, not closing.[70]

There are also numerous voices saying that many colleges and universities, including even prestigious places, are on financially unsustainable paths. Moody's recent "Higher Education Mid-Year Outlook" paints a grim picture of the future of higher education. One of our most esteemed leaders in higher education, Brit Kirwan, has been warning for years that we are indeed in perilous times. Speaking before the AAU in the spring of 2010, he said, "We are also in a period of fiscal famine, experiencing unprecedented resource trauma that threatens the ability of many, if not most of our institutions to carry out their core missions."[71] I agree with Chancellor Kirwan's assessment. But I would add (and I don't think he would disagree) that it is easy, and wrong, to underplay the staying power and resiliency of colleges and universities—a lesson that history teaches us. We should avoid that mistake.

Nor should we blame the "inexorable" workings of the cost disease for whatever grim prospects seem to lie ahead. In a new book, William J. Baumol explains clearly that the same economy-wide increases in productivity that are at the root of the cost disease raise overall wealth and generate additional resources that *could* be used to pay the rising relative costs of activities in labor-intensive sectors such as education, *if* we were to choose to spend them in this way. As Baumol notes in his introduction, this proposition about "possibilities" was first explained to him by the renowned Cambridge economist Joan Robinson many decades ago, but even Baumol did not immediately recognize its full implications. Future prospects come down to a matter of priorities. *Could* is not the same as *will*. The key question, then, is whether we will choose, collectively, to invest the fruits of overall productivity gains on goods such as quality education.[72]

My verdict: not likely. To be sure, in November 2012 voters in California passed "a tax hike that averts what many called potentially disastrous cuts" in state support for higher education.[73] But it is well to remember that this action comes after a series of sharp cuts in state funding, tuition increases, and the imposition of enrollment caps.[74] This is also a special case in that the dire consequences for a great many people, and perhaps for the state overall, of failing to avoid further cuts were spelled out in great detail—and yet the margin of victory was still fairly narrow. Previous cuts were not rescinded, and a bit of breathing room is all that has been achieved.

It seems to me, as to many others, that people in general are fed up with rising costs, and especially rising student charges, however understandable the reasons for them may be. As Baum, Kurose, and McPherson put it in an early version of their "Overview" paper: "The anger and resentment expressed toward college leaders appear to be growing, despite the limited ability of those leaders to make college cheaper quickly without lowering quality in ways that will disappoint the same people who decry higher prices." They added: "Americans as a whole seem extremely reluctant to accept the idea that they should pay more in order to provide more education to more students. Instead the prevalent view seems to be that colleges and universities, especially those in the public sector, should simply find ways to do more with less. If nothing else, sheer political prudence requires colleges to redouble their efforts to accomplish just that, and to undertake those efforts in the most visible possible way."[75]

Otherwise, or in any case, politicians are likely to seek to tie state support to performance goals that may in some cases be overly narrow or short-term in their focus. For example, the governor of Wisconsin has suggested rewarding students for earning degrees "in jobs that are open and needed today," however relevant (or irrelevant) such training for today's jobs may be in the long run.[76]

No part of higher education is immune from the consequences of ignoring this rising tide of anger and resentment. Public perceptions matter, and even seemingly sacrosanct programs such as National Institutes of Health funding for research could be affected if there is spreading distrust of higher education and disbelief in its willingness (commitment?) to "do more with less." Thus, there are self-serving reasons for even privileged institutions such as Stanford and Princeton to pay close attention to these issues. There are also, of course, nobler instincts at play, and I believe, as I will say in the second part of this book, that thoughtfully developed system-wide efforts have the potential not to cure the cost disease but to ease its harshest effects. This will be far from easy. There are no silver bullets in sight. But there is promising work to be done, if only we can muster the *will* to meet challenges that are at least as much organizational and philosophical as they are technical. As John Doar used to say to me in the context of the Nixon impeachment inquiry, which he led, "We will know more later."

## Notes

1. Clark Kerr, foreword to William G. Bowen, *The Economics of the Major Private Universities* (New York: McGraw-Hill, 1968).
2. William J. Baumol and William G. Bowen, *Performing Arts, the Economic Dilemma: A Study of Problems Common to Theater, Opera, Music, and Dance* (New York: Twentieth Century Fund, 1966).
3. Robert H. Frank, "The Prestige Chase Is Raising College Costs," *New York Times*, March 10, 2012. As several commentators have pointed out, it is clear that Frank was referring to only the first movement of Beethoven's String Quartet No. 4 in C minor, Op. 18, which is approximately nine minutes long. The quartet in its entirety is approximately twenty-five minutes long.
4. See Baumol and Bowen, *Performing Arts, the Economic Dilemma*, especially chapters 8 and 9, which document trends in the overall cost of performance, performers' salaries, and other cost components.
5. See William G. Bowen, "The Economics of Princeton in the 1970s: Some Worrisome Implications of Trying to Make Do with Less," Report of the President, February 1976. This report also cites data for Australia (and see Bowen, *The Economics of the Major Private Universities*, for data on the United Kingdom). The cost disease is no respecter of national boundaries. In this report, I also restated the basic cost-disease proposition a bit more fully: "The central economic fact of life is the very nature of the processes of education and scholarship. To be done well, particularly at advanced levels, they require a degree of personal attention and personal interaction that simply do not allow the same opportunities for technological change, mechanization, and, if you will, increases in 'output per unit of labor input,' that characterize the production of such goods as feed grains and calculators. As a result, we must expect the costs and prices of educational services to rise more rapidly than prices in general over the long run." (Bowen, "The Economics of Princeton in the 1970s," 5.) In retrospect, I am especially pleased that I emphasized that the cost disease is a particularly intractable problem at "advanced levels" of teaching.

6. Sandy Baum, Charles Kurose, and Michael S. McPherson, "An Overview of Higher Education," paper presented at *Future of Children* Postsecondary Education in the United States authors' conference, Princeton, NJ, April 26–27, 2012. The study they cite, based on Delta Cost Project data, is Donna M. Desrochers and Jane V. Wellman, "Trends in College Spending, 1999–2009" (Washington, DC: Delta Cost Project, 2011). The "Overview" paper includes a veritable wealth of data on almost every aspect of American higher education over the last fifty years and should be a standard reference. It also contains yet another explanation of the cost disease, and one that is especially detailed—but the paper's authors do not, as I do not, put the onus for rising costs solely on this phenomenon.

The Delta Cost Project, cited extensively in Baum, Kurose, and McPherson's "Overview," has worked with aggregate data available publicly through the Integrated Postsecondary Education Data System. These data in their raw form are not consistent over time, and a real contribution of the Delta Cost Project has been to "clean" the public data and make them consistent. The project has looked at both revenues and expenditures, focusing on public research universities, public master's universities, public community colleges, not-for-profit private research universities, not-for-profit private master's institutions, and not-for-profit private bachelor's institutions; the for-profit sector has not been included because it has been too difficult to obtain consistent data on trends. A good summary of the most recent data is provided in Wellman's testimony before the House Subcommittee on Higher Education; see Jane V. Wellman, Statement to the House, Subcommittee on Higher Education and Workforce Training, Committee on Education and the Workforce, *Keeping College Within Reach: Discussing Ways Institutions Can Streamline Costs and Reduce Tuition*, Hearing, November 30, 2011 (Serial No. 112–48).

Another well-known source of data on costs is a set of studies known as the Delaware Studies. In response to a congressional mandate in the 1998 Higher Education Act, the National Center for Education Statistics (NCES) published three reports, the last of which is Michael F. Middaugh, Rosalinda Graham, and Abdus Shahid, *A Study of Higher Education Instructional Expenditures: The Delaware Study of Instructional Costs and Productivity* (Washington, DC: U.S. Department of Education, National Center for Education Statistics, 2003). Since the publication of that third report, the University of Delaware has continued to survey institutions that volunteer to participate and to give participating institutions their own data, as well as data for sets of comparable institutions (defined by Carnegie classification) so that they can benchmark their own data. These studies are concerned with academic disciplines (such as mathematics). The Delaware Studies also focus on direct instructional expenditures and the factors associated with calculations of direct instructional expenditures per student credit hour (enrollment multiplied by course credits) at four-year colleges and universities. A main finding is that differences among institutions are heavily driven by discipline mix, with costs higher in the sciences than in the humanities. Costs are also related to Carnegie classification (and are higher at research universities) and to variables such as scale.

7. See Christopher Newfield, "Democrats Need a Huge Push to Fix Public Higher Education," *Chronicle of Higher Education,* Conversation blog, November 19, 2012.

8. Teresa A. Sullivan et al., eds., *Improving Measurement of Productivity in Higher Education: Panel on Measuring Higher Education Productivity: Conceptual Framework and Data Needs* (Washington, DC: National Academies Press, 2012), 2. There are also many papers that discuss ways to improve productivity in higher education. See, for example, Davis Jenkins and Olga Rodriguez, "Access and Success for Less: Improving Productivity in Broad-Access Postsecondary Institutions," *The Future of Children* (forthcoming); and Douglas N. Harris and Sara Goldrick-Rab, "The (Un)Productivity of American Higher Education: From 'Cost Disease' to Cost-Effectiveness," WISCAPE Working Paper, December 2010. But these papers have more to say about forces driving up costs (the subject of my next section) than about the measurement of productivity per se.

9. See Spencer S. Jones, Paul S. Heaton, Robert S. Rudin, and Eric C. Schneider, "Unraveling the IT Productivity Paradox—Lessons for Health Care," *New England Journal of Medicine* 366 (June 14, 2012): 2243–45.

10. Ibid., 2243.

11. Ibid., 2244.

12. See William G. Bowen and Derek Bok, *The Shape of the River: Long-Term Consequences of Considering Race in College and University Admissions* (Princeton, NJ: Princeton University Press, 1998).

13. Kevin M. Guthrie, founding president of JSTOR and now president of ITHAKA (which encompasses JSTOR), points out that, thanks to JSTOR, there is now some work that gets done that never would have been done before—as a result, for example, of finding old literature that otherwise would have been inaccessible—thus adding to the numerator of the productivity ratio. Similarly, universities in places like South Africa now have access to both literature (via JSTOR) and art images (via ARTstor) that otherwise never would have been possible.

14. During the discussion session following the presentation of this lecture, President Hennessy contributed a short list of other factors that he believed, on the basis of his experience at Stanford, to have contributed to rising costs. These included increases in state Medicaid obligations as a proportion of state budgets, which can crowd out appropriations for higher education (see Thomas J. Kane, Peter R. Orszag, and David L. Gunter, "State Fiscal Constraints and Higher Education Spending: The Role of Medicaid and the Business Cycle," Tax Policy Center, May 2003, http://taxpolicycenter.org/publications/url.cfm?ID=310787); increases in expenditures on student mental health costs; increases in the proportion of low-income and first-generation college students at universities such as Stanford;

and increases in initiatives like community centers and ethnic-themed dorms that Hennessy believes have helped improve Stanford's completion rate.

15. *Forbes,* November 19, 2012.

16. For a summary of Bain's work on these campuses, see Kevin Kiley, "Where Universities Can Be Cut," *Inside Higher Ed,* September 16, 2011. Also see Jeff Denneen and Tom Dretler, *The Financially Sustainable University* (Bain & Company and Sterling Partners, 2012), www.bain.com/Images/BAIN_BRIEF_The_financially_sustainable_university.pdf. The McKinsey consulting firm has been active in this area as well; see, for instance, Byron G. Auguste, Adam Cota, Kartik Jayaram, and Martha C. A. Laboissière, *Winning by Degrees: The Strategies of Highly Productive Higher Education Institutions* (McKinsey & Company, November 2010), http://mckinseyonsociety.com/downloads/reports/Education/Winning%20by%20degrees%20report%20fullreport%20v5.pdf.

17. In a lengthy front-page story in the *Wall Street Journal,* Douglas Belkin and Scott Thurm analyze data for the University of Minnesota to make the case that inefficiencies and a growing bureaucracy have been largely responsible for increasing costs. (Douglas Belkin and Scott Thurm, "Deans List: Hiring Spree Fattens College Bureaucracy—and Tuition," *Wall Street Journal,* December 29, 2012.) In considering this argument, it is wise to remember that the University of Minnesota may be an outlier in some respects; for example, as the authors point out, data compiled by the U.S. Department of Education show that, among the seventy-two "very-high-research" public universities in the 2011–12 academic year, the University's main Twin Cities campus had the largest proportion of "executive/administrative and managerial" employees. Not all public institutions have experienced what is sometimes described as an increase in "administrative bloat." For example, the University of Nebraska, according to a *Chronicle of Higher Education* article published less than two weeks later, has seen a 5 percent decline in the number of employees with administrative faculty positions between 2001 and 2012.

At the same time, however, Jane Wellman, currently executive director of the National Association of System Heads and formerly head of the Delta Cost Project, notes that the costs of employing more administrators amount to too small a proportion of universities' overall budgets to account for recent tuition increases or higher education costs; even the University of Minnesota's costs of administrative oversight constitute only 9 percent of its expenditures. In addition, it is important to ask what fraction of the increases in non-instructional costs at Minnesota can be attributed to the growth in research programs over the period in question—probably a high fraction. For example, Minnesota's technology, research, communications, and student-services staffs increased "significant[ly]" over the past thirteen years, and research staff at the University of Nebraska doubled as its research expenditures increased from $136 million to $232 million between 2000 and 2011. (Belkin and Thurm, "Deans List"; Jenny Rogers, "How

Many Administrators Are Too Many?" *Chronicle of Higher Education,* January 7, 2013.)

18. When I was president of the Andrew W. Mellon Foundation, I resolutely opposed the creation of new "centers" unless there was an overwhelming case for them. The University of Chicago has been an especially creative user of the "workshop" model, which stresses the value of *temporary* groupings of faculty and students. Tufts University has had excellent results with the use of the "experimental college" to test out curricular experiments without making more than one-year commitments.

19. For an extended discussion of these issues, written by two veteran leaders of public-university business schools, see Gary C. Fethke and Andrew J. Policano, *Public No More: A New Path to Excellence for America's Public Universities* (Stanford, CA: Stanford University Press, 2012), especially chapters 7, 8, and 12. The controversy at the University of Virginia in spring 2012 over the leadership of President Teresa Sullivan also involved aspects of this debate (how important is it for U.Va. to teach German?). See Scott Jaschik, "Fired for Protecting Languages?" *Inside Higher Ed,* June 18, 2012. Of course, it is easy to state such issues in overly simple terms. For example, it is one thing to insist that U.Va. must continue to be a leader in the teaching of German but quite another to insist that many separate language departments are essential. Precisely how worthy educational objectives are to be served is a legitimate question, which I raise here without suggesting an answer.

20. See Charles T. Clotfelter, *Buying the Best: Cost Escalation in Elite Higher Education* (Princeton, NJ: Princeton University Press, 1996). Clotfelter looks at the economic factors that drive actions by institutions of higher education and examines the escalation in spending in the arts and sciences at four elite institutions: Harvard, Duke, the University of Chicago, and Carleton College. He argues that the rise in costs has less to do with increasing faculty salaries or decreasing productivity than with broad-based efforts to improve quality, provide new services to students, pay for large investments in new facilities and equipment (including computers), and ensure access for low-income students through increasingly expensive financial aid.

21. For an early presentation of this line of argument, see Howard Bowen's discussion of the revenue theory of cost in his *The Cost of Higher Education* (San Francisco: Jossey-Bass, 1980).

22. Lawrence S. Bacow, personal communication, November 22, 2011.

23. Even among the most prestigious universities in the nation, there is a dramatic difference in endowments, which has grown, in absolute terms, over the past ten years. In fiscal year 2001, for instance, Harvard's endowment was about $18 billion, and those of Yale and Princeton were $10.7 billion and $8.4 billion, respectively. By contrast, in that fiscal year Columbia had an endowment of $4.2 billion, and the University of Pennsylvania and the University of Chicago had endowments of $3.4 billion and $3.3 billion, respectively. By fiscal year 2011, Harvard's endowment

was $31.7 billion, and those of Yale and Princeton had grown to $19.4 billion and $17.1 billion, respectively. In comparison, the endowments of Columbia, the University of Pennsylvania, and the University of Chicago were each in the $6 billion to $8 billion range. See National Association of College and University Business Officers, *NACUBO Endowment Study, 2002*, and *NACUBO-Commonfund Study of Endowments, 2011*, both available at www.nacubo.org/Research/NACUBO-Commonfund_ Study_ of_Endowments/Public_NCSE_Tables_.html.

For an excellent discussion of stratification more generally, and the forces driving it, see Caroline M. Hoxby, "The Changing Selectivity of American Colleges," *Journal of Economic Perspectives* 23, no. 4 (2009), especially pp. 95–96 and 98. Hoxby concentrates on stratification by student achievement and notes that only the top 10 percent of colleges were substantially more selective in 2007 than they were in 1962. Most colleges became less selective over this period. Hoxby also explains how student selectivity and educational expenditures interact.

24. President Catherine Hill from Vassar spoke eloquently at the April 2012 Lafayette Conference on the Future of the Liberal Arts College on the pressure that selective institutions feel to meet the perceived needs and desires of students from affluent families. Also telling is a recent article in the *Atlantic* about former George Washington University president Stephen Trachtenberg, who, between 1988 and 2007, built not only computer and research labs but also a "profusion of comforts [that] didn't just stimulate students' minds; they also fulfilled their every whim—a change that drew a more selective, more intelligent group of applicants and sent the admission rate plummeting from 75 percent to 37 percent." Unsurprisingly, these new amenities caused tuition to double during the term of his presidency (after inflation is taken into account). The article continues: " 'It was a matter of competition,' Trachtenberg says in the way of justifying the suite-style dorms he built, the remote campus he acquired, and the tuition hikes that he began almost immediately. 'These sorts of facilities were being offered elsewhere. We were either in the game or we weren't in the game.' " (Julia Edwards, "Meet the High Priest of Runaway College Inflation (He Regrets Nothing)," *Atlantic*, September 30, 2012.)

25. See William G. Bowen, Matthew M. Chingos, and Michael S. McPherson, *Crossing the Finish Line: Completing College at America's Public Universities* (Princeton, NJ: Princeton University Press, 2009), especially chapter 6, for striking evidence that performance-based indicators, such as class rank and achievement test scores, are far better predictors than aptitude tests like the SAT of almost everything—except family wealth! Preoccupation with yield is also troubling. I can't count the number of times at Princeton that I told the admissions office that I didn't want to hear anything about yield; what matters, I did my best to explain, is the quality and character of the incoming class, not how many promising students elected to go elsewhere.

26. The quotation was provided by a former colleague of mine at the Andrew W. Mellon Foundation, Idana Goldberg.

27. As president of Princeton, I led an effort within the Ivy League to create and apply an "academic index" to govern admissions requirements. It had some good effects, but it also had some undesirable side effects that I did not understand until much later. (See William G. Bowen and Sarah Levin, *Reclaiming the Game* [Princeton, NJ: Princeton University Press, 2008].)

28. Institutions can no longer require tenured faculty members to retire at age 70 (as was possible before 1994). As a result, "I can stay forever," Ronald Ehrenberg, a tenured faculty member and director of the Cornell Higher Education Research Institute at Cornell University, recently told *Inside Higher Ed.* This situation can prove frustrating and expensive for tenure-granting administrators. One university president at a highly renowned private university lamented having to spend millions of dollars on buying out superannuated and unproductive faculty members who are reluctant to retire. (Colleen Flaherty, "Adjunct Leaders Consider Strategies to Force Change," *Inside Higher Ed,* January 9, 2013.)

29. William G. Bowen and Neil L. Rudenstine, *In Pursuit of the PhD* (Princeton, NJ: Princeton University Press, 1992).

30. See Robert M. Berdahl, "Reassessing the Value of Research Universities," *Chronicle of Higher Education,* July 13, 2009.

31. See Paul Basken, "Nation's Research Universities Are Offered Hope of Fatter Budgets—at a Price," *Chronicle of Higher Education,* June 14, 2012.

32. During the discussion session following the original delivery of this lecture, President Hennessy was very direct in saying that the United States is producing too many PhD's and that we are going to have to accept the fact that in the future there will be fewer faculty positions than there are today. That being said, a relatively wealthy university like Stanford will probably be better able to finance its graduate programs in the future than many less-well-off public and private institutions. Still, it is unlikely that Stanford will remain completely insulated from pressures to economize.

33. See John Bound, Michael F. Lovenheim, and Sarah Turner, "Increasing Time to Baccalaureate Degree in the United States," National Bureau of Economic Research, Working Paper 15892, April 2010. Also see the discussion of this study in Baum, Kurose, and McPherson, "Overview." Of course, college readiness is also part of the problem. The low rate of college readiness among high school graduates in, for example, New York is certainly troubling. (See Sharon Otterman, "College-Readiness Low among State Graduates, Data Show," *New York Times,* June 14, 2011.)

34. Focusing on completion rates and time-to-degree reminds us of the dangers of looking only (or mainly) at measures of "cost per [enrolled] student." There is much to be said for examining "cost per degree conferred," though here again care is needed to avoid treating all degrees as the same or assigning no value at all to learning that does not result in a degree.

35. See Bowen, Chingos, and McPherson, *Crossing the Finish Line,* especially chapter 4. It is Matthew M. Chingos who deserves the credit for this part of the analysis. Similarly, a *Chronicle of Higher Education* article reports that "many students take far more credits than they need to earn a degree" and thus stay in school longer than necessary. (Eric Kelderman, "Board Suggests Ways for Southern States to Lower College Costs and Increase Degree Production," *Chronicle of Higher Education,* September 28, 2010.) A significant source of the problem is blocked passages to degrees. A survey conducted by the chancellor's office of the California Community Colleges system in late August 2012 revealed that more than 472,000 of the system's 2.4 million students were put on waiting lists for fall 2012 classes. (See Lee Gardner, "Survey of California Community Colleges Reveals Drastic Effects of Budget Cuts," *Chronicle of Higher Education,* August 29, 2012.)

36. See Bowen, Chingos, and McPherson, *Crossing the Finish Line,* 237.

37. See Daniel de Vise, "Public Universities Pushing Super-Seniors to the Graduation Stage," *Washington Post,* June 2, 2012. Other imaginative efforts have been made to attack this problem. Lawrence S. Bacow, former president of Tufts, has reported that Tufts had success with a modest program of grants that allowed the neediest students to attend summer school between junior and senior year (something that wealthier students often do without institutional help).

38. In June 2011 the trustees of the City University of New York (CUNY) approved a resolution creating the Pathways initiative, which is designed to facilitate the transfer process between the system's two- and four-year colleges. Under this project, all students in the system are required to complete thirty "Common Core" credits; students who are transferring from community to senior colleges are required to take an additional six to twelve "College Option" credits. Individual colleges have substantial flexibility in determining the content of the "Common Core" credits, and, in the case of the senior colleges, the College Option credits. For more information on the Pathways Initiative, see www.cuny.edu/academics/initiatives/degreepathways.html, accessed August 30, 2012.

39. See chapter 5 of Bowen, Chingos, and McPherson, *Crossing the Finish Line,* for an extended discussion of the concept of matching and the phenomenon of undermatching in North Carolina, and p. 99 in particular for a description of the important work of the Chicago Consortium in that city.

40. Ibid., especially chapter 10 and pp. 233–35. Hard as we worked to control for selection effects in this study, a new paper by Sarah Cohodes and Joshua Goodman controls for selection effects even more convincingly by using a research discontinuity design and working with rich data from a Massachusetts Merit Aid program. The authors find that students induced by this scholarship program to attend less selective colleges were more than 40 percent less likely to graduate. They also find that "students are remarkably willing to forego college quality for relatively small amounts of

money." (Sarah Cohodes and Joshua Goodman, "First Degree Earns: The Impact of College Quality on College Completion Rates," Harvard Kennedy School Working Paper Series RWP12-033, August 7, 2012.) The classic (crisp) discussion of returns to selectivity is Hoxby, "Changing Selectivity," especially pp. 114–15. Hoxby emphasizes that colleges and universities that attract high-achieving students also invest more in "student-oriented resources"—which is, of course, an important reason that so many students with strong qualifications go to these schools.

41. For a description of the MDRC study and a policy brief explaining the context of the project, see Jay Sherwin, "Make Me a Match: Helping Low-Income and First-Generation Students Make Good College Choices," MDRC, March 2012, www.mdrc.org/publications/623/overview.html. For a description of the Hoxby-Turner project, see "About the Expanding College Opportunities (ECO) Project," Expanding College Opportunities, www.expandingcollegeopps.org/eco/about, accessed August 29, 2012. One reader of a draft of this Tanner Lecture suggested that lessons might also be learned from matching programs for medical students.

42. Some have wondered if improving "match" would just substitute more-qualified students for less-qualified students at certain institutions, leaving overall enrollments (and perhaps overall graduation rates) unchanged. This is a good question, and it is surely true that there would probably be no significant effects on overall completion rates at highly selective institutions. But we are not really interested in the Harvards of the world in this context, and I suspect that there is more elasticity in the capacity of moderately selective institutions than is sometimes understood—especially when we recognize that reducing time-to-degree increases the number of students who can be accommodated with a given number of classroom seats. We should also be aware, however, that these moderately selective institutions might have difficulty meeting the financial aid needs of larger numbers of students from modest family circumstances. More thought also needs to be given to the likely effects of any displacement of some students that might occur as a result of better matching. Since there is evidence that it is precisely the kinds of students currently "undermatched" who benefit most from attending institutions with challenging academic programs, it is certainly possible that some reshuffling of the student population could, in and of itself, improve overall completion rates and time-to-degree—and thus productivity. It is also true that such reshuffling might be hard to manage politically, its appeal on the merits notwithstanding.

43. To move from an analysis of institutional costs in higher education to a discussion of affordability for students and their families requires us to peel several layers off the proverbial onion. First, students in nonprofit institutions of all kinds are almost never expected to pay the full costs of their education. State appropriations, federal grants, private gifts, earnings from endowments, and earned income are other sources of revenue which drive a wedge between costs and tuition. Nearly all students in the nonprofit sector receive subsidies,

which are often non-trivial in size. Second, thanks to financial aid and "discounts," there is often a sizeable difference between quoted tuition ("sticker price") and what students actually pay ("net tuition"). Third, affordability depends not just on what a student is expected to pay, but on trends in family income and wealth that, in turn, depend on variables external to higher education. Finally, it can be difficult to calibrate the long-run effects of different choices that students and parents make in deciding how to pay their college bills, including how much to borrow and what forms of debt make the most sense. Difficulties involved in making these distinctions are compounded by huge differences in tuition levels across higher education and the tendency of journalists to pay far too much attention to stated charges at elite private institutions that enroll only a small fraction of students. Also, it has proved difficult for prospective students and their families to understand widely differing financial aid policies and to recognize that in many cases they will be asked to pay far less than the sticker price.

44. Aggregating data for all state systems, a report by the State Higher Education Executive Officers tells us: "In 2010, state and locally financed educational appropriations for public higher education hit the lowest level ($6,532 per FTE [full-time equivalent enrollment] in constant 2011 dollars) in a quarter century.... This downward trend continued in 2011 with state and locally financed educational appropriations at $6,290 per FTE, a decline of 3.7 percent over 2010 in constant dollars." The report adds that appropriations per FTE would have been even lower, "except for budget driven enrollment caps in some states and reductions in state financial assistance." (State Higher Education Executive Officers, *State Higher Education Finance, FY 2011,* 2012, 19; see also ibid., 20, figure 3.)

45. See Sandy Baum, Charles Kurose, and Michael S. McPherson, "An Overview of Higher Education," *Future of Children* 23, no. 1 (2013).

46. See Rajashri Chakrabarti, Maricar Mabutas, and Basit Zafar, "Soaring Tuitions: Are Public Funding Cuts to Blame?" Federal Reserve Bank of New York, September 19, 2012, http://libertystreeteconomics .newyorkfed.org/2012/09/soaring-tuitions-are-public-funding-cuts-to-blame .html#.UFnZJAauLvQ.twitter, which reports that increases in net tuition at public institutions have been associated with decreases in state and local appropriations since 2007.

47. See Sandy Baum and Jennifer Ma, *Trends in College Pricing* (New York: College Board, 2012).

48. Ibid., 7.

49. See State Higher Education Executive Officers, *State Higher Education Finance, FY 2011.*

50. Joseph E. Stiglitz, "Debt Buries Graduates' American Dream," *USA Today Weekly, International Edition,* July 13–15, 2012. Survey data confirm that over the past four years, students have started to foot an increasing share of their families' total expenditures on college. Between the 2008–09 and the 2011–12 academic years, the share of family college

expenditures paid for by parents' borrowing, income, and savings has fallen from 40 percent to 37 percent, at the same time as the share of the expenditures contributed by the students' borrowing, income, and savings has risen from 24 percent to 30 percent. See Sallie Mae and Ipsos, *How America Pays for College* (Newark, DE: Sallie Mae, 2012), 8; in addition, the pie chart on p. 7 of this report shows the share of expenses paid from various sources, including savings, grants and scholarships, contributions by relatives, and borrowing by both students and their parents.

51. The results of the most recent administration of the National Survey of Student Engagement (NSSE) are similarly encouraging in this regard: about three-quarters of students in their freshman and senior years agreed that college was a good investment. See National Survey of Student Engagement, *Promoting Student Learning and Institutional Improvement: Lessons from NSSE at 13: Annual Results 2012* (Bloomington: Indiana University Center for Postsecondary Research, 2012), 17.

52. See Sallie Mae and Ipsos, *How America Pays for College*, 14, 40. This is not the place to review the vast literature on returns to education, but I believe many commentators (including, unfortunately, many of those speaking for colleges and universities) put too much emphasis on purely economic returns, important as they are. Years ago, in the midst of the depression of the 1930s, no less a figure than the conservative Chicago economist Frank Knight cautioned against over-emphasis on the virtues of what he called "the business game." He observed: "However favorable an opinion one may hold of the business game, he must be very illiberal not to concede that others have a right to a different view and that large numbers of admirable people do not like the game at all. It is then justifiable at least to regard as unfortunate the dominance of the business game over life, the virtual identification of social living with it, to the extent that has come to pass in the modern world." (Frank H. Knight, *The Ethics of Competition* [New Brunswick, NJ: Transaction, 2009], 58.) Also see Sandy Baum, Jennifer Ma, and Kathleen Payea, *Education Pays, 2010* (New York: College Board Advocacy & Policy Center, 2010), for a useful summary of the benefits higher education confers, on individuals and society in general, beyond earnings effects.

53. Economists are strong believers in revealed preferences, and it would be most helpful to see what students actually do, not simply what they say they want to do or even what they say that they will do. In contemplating research on such questions, it is important to recognize that it is not enough to focus just on "average" net tuition. Much depends on the distribution of both need-based aid and merit aid by type of student and type of institution attended. What is required is detailed data at the student level that can be connected to institutional data—and such data are hard to obtain for defined populations of students attending different kinds of colleges and universities in various states. National panel data are generally too highly aggregated to serve this purpose.

54. See Josh Mitchell, "Student Debt Rises by 8% as College Tuitions Climb," *Wall Street Journal,* May 31, 2012. This article cites data from the Federal Reserve Bank of New York; the online edition also presents a vivid graphic showing the decline in credit card debt alongside the rapid growth in student debt.

55. Andrew Martin and Andrew W. Lehren, "A Generation Hobbled by the Soaring Cost of College," *New York Times,* May 12, 2012, online edition.

56. See Sandy Baum and Michael McPherson, "The New York Times Blunder," *Chronicle of Higher Education,* May 17, 2012. As Baum and McPherson point out, citing Sarah Turner, the source of the error was incompetent analysis of Department of Education data (failing to understand a skip pattern and ignoring correct data which was supplied to the authors by the Department of Education). What is most disconcerting is that the number reported in the *Times* article didn't pass any semblance of a "smell test"; Baum and McPherson surmise that the "story seemed to be striving for maximum drama rather than for an accurate picture of student debt and the very real problems it creates for too many students." An even deeper lesson to be gleaned from this fiasco is that there is a terrible lack of sophistication among many journalists (though certainly not all) covering higher education—a point that Nicholas Lemann, dean of the School of Journalism at Columbia University, has made repeatedly.

57. Baum and McPherson, "The New York Times Blunder."

58. Matthew M. Chingos, personal communication, May 13, 2012.

59. Christopher Avery and Sarah Turner, "Student Loans: Do College Students Borrow Too Much—or Not Enough?" *Journal of Economic Perspectives* 26, no. 1 (Winter 2012): 1–30.

60. Ibid., 25.

61. See Bowen, Chingos, and McPherson, *Crossing the Finish Line,* 163–64. Similarly, the most recent NSSE results showed that about 32 percent of freshmen and 36 percent of seniors reported that financial concerns had interfered with their academic performance; this proportion rose to almost 60 percent for full-time seniors who worked twenty-one or more hours per week. About three in ten freshmen and seniors also said they often chose not to purchase required academic materials because of their cost, and more than four in ten reported they often chose not to participate in an activity due to lack of money. (National Survey of Student Engagement, *Promoting Student Learning,* 17.)

62. This figure comes from the Baccalaureate and Beyond data set, collected by the Department of Education's National Center on Education Statistics, which provides data on the cumulative student loan balances as of 2009 for the graduating class of 2008. (See also Mitchell, "Student Debt Rises by 8%," and Jennifer Cohen and Jason Delisle, "Focusing the Student Loan Conversation on the Average Borrower, Not the Average Loan," *Ed Money Watch,* New America Foundation, May 15, 2012, http://edmoney

.newamerica.net/blogposts/2012/focusing_the_student_loan_conversation_ on_the_average_borrower_not_the_average_loan-6.) NCES data also show that, of students who began their undergraduate education in 2003–04 and who had attained a certificate, associate's degree, or bachelor's degree by 2008–09, 62 percent had borrowed for their undergraduate education, and the average cumulative amount borrowed by those students was $21,700 (in 2012 dollars). For more information about student debt, see Christina Chang Wei, Lutz Berkner, and C. Dennis Carroll, *Trends in Undergraduate Borrowing II: Federal Student Loans in 1995–96, 1999–2000, and 2003– 04*, NCES 2008–179rev (Washington, DC: U.S. Department of Education, National Center for Education Statistics, Institute of Education Sciences, 2008), http://nces.ed.gov/pubs2008/2008179rev.pdf.

63. Richard Fry, *A Record One-in-Five Households Now Owe Student Loan Debt,* Pew Research Center, September 26, 2012, www .pewsocialtrends.org/2012/09/26/a-record-one-in-five-households-now -owe-student-loan-debt/.

64. See Jesse Rothstein and Cecilia Rouse, "Constrained after College: Student Loans and Early Career Occupational Choices," *Journal of Public Economics* 95, no. 1–2 (2012): 149–63, cited in Avery and Turner's "Student Loans." As part of the College Cost Reduction and Access Act of 2007, the government enacted an income-based repayment (IBR) program for students who have high levels of debt relative to their income and/or who are pursuing careers in fields with relatively low salaries, such as public service. IBR caps students' monthly repayments on federal student loans according to their discretionary income level. The maximum repayment period under this program is twenty-five years, after which students' remaining debt is forgiven. The 2007 law also established a loan-forgiveness program particularly for students who pursue careers in public service. Under this program, any remaining debt is discharged after borrowers have worked full-time in public service for ten years and have made 120 monthly payments on an eligible Federal Direct Loan. Unlike IBR's twenty-five-year forgiveness program, the ten-year public-service forgiveness program is tax-free. For more information, see Mark Kantrowitz, "Income-Based Repayment," FinAid, 2012, www.finaid.org/ibr; and Mark Kantrowitz, "Public Service Loan Forgiveness," FinAid, 2012, www.finaid.org/loans/ publicservice.phtml.

65. See Bowen and Bok, *The Shape of the River.*

66. Ibid., introduction to the paperback edition, especially p. xxxix.

67. Matthew M. Chingos, Michael S. McPherson, and I would like to claim some credit for this shift in emphasis from enrollment to degree completion. See *Crossing the Finish Line.*

68. See Coffin Eaton, "At White House Meeting on Affordability, a Call for Urgency, Innovation, and Leadership," *Chronicle of Higher Education,* December 5, 2011; "Reining in College Tuition," *New York Times,* February 3, 2012. Several of the university leaders present at the

White House meeting as well as the *Times* editorial board agree with President Obama that "the federal government must do more to rein in tuition costs at the public colleges that educate more than 70 percent of the nation's students" ("Reining in College Tuition").

69. In 2009, for instance, only about 40 percent of 25- to 34-year-olds in the United States had attained some form of tertiary education, giving the United States a rank of sixteenth in the world, according to the Organization for Economic Co-operation and Development. By contrast, among adults between the ages of 55 and 64, the United States' rate of higher-education attainment was also about 40 percent, giving it a rank of third in the world for this age group and making it virtually the only G20 nation whose rate of attainment had not grown between the older and the younger cohorts. See Organization for Economic Co-operation and Development, *Education at a Glance, 2011,* September 13, 2011, doi: 10.1787/19991487.

70. See studies by Sean F. Reardon at Stanford and Susan M. Dynarski and Martha J. Bailey at the University of Michigan, among others, in *Whither Opportunity? Rising Inequality, Schools, and Children's Life Chances,* ed. Greg J. Duncan and Richard J. Murnane (New York: Russell Sage Foundation and Spencer Foundation, 2011). A recent article in the *New York Times* offers poignant anecdotes of three young women in Texas whose precarious financial circumstances, in combination with other challenges in their personal lives, have interfered with their ability to earn four-year college degrees. The article cites research by Chingos showing that even students from low-income families who earn higher test scores than their wealthier classmates still complete college at lower rates, as well as Reardon's finding that the difference between high- and low-income students' scores has grown by 40 percent in the last quarter century. (Jason DeParle, "For Poor, Leap to College Often Ends in Hard Fall," *New York Times,* December 23, 2012.)

As Jeff Selingo has warned, enrollment caps in states such as California may be at least as serious a problem as reductions in appropriations, since some students, especially those from modest backgrounds, may be deprived of any in-state enrollment option in the public university sector. (Jeff Selingo, "For Have-Nots, the Rockier Road to a College Degree Increases the Appeal of Alternatives," *Chronicle of Higher Education,* March 23, 2012.) Selingo worries that enrollment caps and other large disruptions in the higher education system "could worsen the divide between the haves and have-nots." He cites two examples of such disruptions, including Western Governors University—a nonprofit institution at which students work through course materials, many of which are available online, at their own pace, and earn credit by demonstrating their mastery of course content on standardized examinations—and MITx—an organization offering not-for-credit online courses taught by MIT professors, currently free of charge, to the general public. Selingo reports that he has never heard any of the critics of the value of traditional higher education say that "they'd surely send their kids to Western Governors University or choose a certificate from MITx over a degree from nearly any four-year college."

71. See William E. Kirwan, "The Research University of the Future," speech at AAU Public Affairs Network Meeting, Washington, DC, March 22, 2010. Kirwan went on to note: "We have, of course, experienced periods of fiscal decline in the past, one as recent as the early part of this decade. But, *this* decline has a different character. In the past, economic downturns were followed by periods of economic boom and losses were recovered relatively quickly. I know no one who predicts that will be the case with our current fiscal decline." Kirwan then commented on "the disconnect between the aspirational rhetoric at the national level and the reality on the ground" by observing that, in a single week, "President Obama announced his laudable goal for leadership in higher education completion rates and Charlie Reed, Chancellor of the California State University System, announced that Cal State was turning away 30,000 students this spring because of inadequate funding." This under-appreciated talk is well worth reading in its entirety. Gary Fethke and Andrew J. Policano agree with Kirwan that "the diminished role of state government funding is permanent" (Fethke and Policano, *Public No More: A New Path to Excellence for America's Public Universities* [Stanford, CA: Stanford University Press, 2012], 218). For another sobering assessment of what might happen to colleges and universities, see Jeff Selingo, "The Fiscal Cliff for Higher Education," *Chronicle of Higher Education,* August 12, 2012. Selingo describes a possible "death spiral" for some institutions, and he seems to be referring especially to lower-rated private colleges—which are definitely threatened by increased competition from lower-priced educational options. I suspect that my colleagues and I, in our focus on the large public university systems, have paid inadequate attention to the problems facing the regional private institutions.

72. See William J. Baumol, *The Cost Disease* (New Haven, CT: Yale University Press, 2012), especially chapter 4.

73. Kevin Kiley, "Californians Approve Measure That Will Avert Major Education Cuts," *Inside Higher Ed,* November 7, 2012.

74. Jonathan Medina, "California Cuts Threaten the Status of Universities," *New York Times,* June 1, 2012.

75. See Baum, Kurose, and McPherson, "Overview."

76. See Dee J. Hall and Samara Kalk Derby, "Gov. Scott Walker Unveils Agenda for Wisconsin During Speech in California," *Wisconsin State Journal,* November 19, 2012. Other states that, with encouragement from the Obama administration, are using performance measures rather than enrollment as the primary determinant of higher education funding include Indiana, Ohio, and, most prominently, Tennessee. (See Joanne Jacobs, "More States Utilize Performance Funding for Higher Education," *U.S. News,* February 24, 2012.)

# Part 2

## Prospects for an Online Fix

HAVING PROVIDED WHAT I hope is a useful context, I will now discuss the prospects for using new technologies to address the productivity, cost, and affordability issues that I have described. I regard the prospects as promising, but also challenging. To succeed we will need to adopt a system-wide perspective, be relentless in seeking evidence about outcomes and costs, change some of our mindsets and our decision-making processes, and exhibit more patience than is our wont. None of these conditions is easy to satisfy! My focus will be on the contributions from established universities already serving large numbers of students. To be sure, we also want to serve new populations, at home and abroad, and a worldwide diffusion of knowledge is a most worthy goal—but it is not my central subject. Finally, in the search for new approaches, we need to recognize how well we do some things now, and how important it is that our educational institutions continue to stand for core values. That is the note on which I will end.

I am not a futurist but rather a maddeningly practical person who rarely has visions—and when I do, they are usually the result of having had a bad meal! But let me put such predilections to one side and ask readers to join me in imagining, just for a moment, how the intelligent harnessing of information technology through the medium of online learning might alter aspects of university life as we know it. Can we imagine a university in which

- faculty collaborate more on teaching (with technology serving as the forcing function)?
- faculty devote more of their time to promoting "active learning" by their students and are freed from much of the tedium of grading and even giving essentially the same lecture countless times?
- students receive more, and more timely, individualized feedback on assignments?
- instruction is guided by evidence drawn from massive amounts of data on how students learn, what mistakes students commonly make, and how misunderstandings underlying those mistakes can be corrected ("adaptive learning")?
- technology is used to bring the perspectives of a more diverse student body onto its campus through its capacity to engage students from around the world?
- technology extends the educational process throughout one's life through the educational equivalent of booster shots? And, ideally:
- a university in which institutional costs and tuition charges rise at a slower rate?

**Background**

Before considering how nirvana might at least be approached (reaching nirvana will take a very long time, if indeed we can ever reach what has to be an ever-changing, ever-more ambitious goal), I want to describe briefly the evolution of my own thinking about technology and online learning. This story dates back at least as far as the Romanes Lecture that I gave at

Oxford in 2000. In that lecture, I stressed the need to be realistic in thinking about how technology impacts costs, and I cited an early study from the University of Illinois that concluded: "Sound online instruction is likely to cost more than traditional instruction."[1] I then cited a supporting observation from another early study: "A cyberprofessor trades the 'chains' of lecturing in a classroom for a predictable number of hours at a specific time and place for the more unpredictable 'freedom' of being accessible by email and other cyber technologies. . . . Many cybercourse instructors find themselves being drawn into an endless time drain."[2] My conclusion at that time: "All the talk of using technology to 'save money by increasing productivity' has a hollow ring in the ears of the budget officer who has to pay for the salaries of a cadre of support staff, more and more equipment, and new software licenses—and who sees few offsetting savings."[3]

I next added the not-so-profound thought that "this could change." I am today a convert. I have come to believe that now is the time. Far greater access to the Internet, improvements in Internet speed, reductions in storage costs, the proliferation of increasingly sophisticated mobile devices, and other advances have combined with changing mindsets to suggest that online learning, in many of its manifestations, can lead to at least comparable learning outcomes relative to face-to-face instruction at lower cost. The phrase *in many of its manifestations* is important. Much confusion can result from failing to recognize that "online learning" is far from one thing—and that online learning is anything but static.[4] It is, in fact, so many things and is evolving so rapidly that the efforts my colleague Kelly Lack and I made to create an understandable taxonomy did not succeed. We felt as if we were trying to "tether a broomstick,"[5] and we decided to content ourselves with describing some distinguishing aspects of this complex landscape. (See the appendix at the end of this part.)

A far more sophisticated observer of digital trends than I am, President John Hennessy of Stanford, has been quoted as saying: "There's a tsunami coming. [But] I can't tell you exactly how it's going to break."[6] Since I live on the East Coast, not the West Coast, I am even less capable of judging tsunamis, their shape, their force, or their timing, but I too am convinced that online learning *could* be truly transformative.

What needs to be done in order to translate *could* into *will?* The principal barriers to overcome can be grouped under three headings: the lack of hard evidence about both learning outcomes and potential cost savings; the lack of shared but customizable teaching and learning platforms (or tool kits); and the need for both new mindsets and fresh thinking about models of decision-making.[7]

## The Lack of Hard Evidence

Prominent leaders in higher education have made it abundantly clear that the faculty and leadership of many institutions, especially those regarded as trend-setters, will consider major changes in how they teach if, and only if, much more hard evidence about potential gains is available. To be sure, better "facts" will not suffice to bring about change, but evidence may well be a necessary if not a sufficient condition.

How effective has online learning been in improving (or at least maintaining) learning outcomes achieved by various populations of students in various settings? Unfortunately, no one really knows the answer to either this question or the important follow-on query about cost savings. There have been literally thousands of studies of online learning, and my colleague, Kelly Lack, has continued to catalogue them and summarize their findings.[8] This has proved to be a daunting task—and, it has to be said, a discouraging one. Very few of these studies are relevant to the teaching of undergraduates, and the few that are relevant almost always suffer from serious methodological deficiencies.[9] The most common problems are small sample size; inability to control for ubiquitous selection effects; and, on the cost side, the lack of good estimates of likely cost savings in steady state.

Ms. Lack and I originally thought that full responsibility for this state of affairs rested with those who conducted the studies. We have revised that judgment. A significant share of responsibility rests with those who have created and used the online pedagogies, since the content often does not lend itself to rigorous assessment, and offerings are rarely designed with evaluation in mind. Moreover, the gold-standard methodology—randomized trials—is both expensive and excruciatingly difficult to implement on university campuses. Also at play is what I can only call the missionary spirit. The creators of many online courses are true believers who simply want to get on with their work, without being distracted by the need to do careful assessments of outcomes or costs. In all fairness, I have to add that these are early days, and it is unrealistic to expect to have in hand today careful assessments of potentially path-breaking offerings such as some of the MOOCs (massive open online courses) that have been introduced relatively recently.[10] Still, there is no excuse for not working now on plans for rigorous third-party evaluations.[11]

As Derek Bok has for years reminded everyone who will listen, the lack of careful studies of the learning effectiveness of various teaching methods is a long-standing problem; it predates and extends well beyond assessments of online learning. With typical candor, Professor William J. Baumol has observed: "In our teaching activity we proceed without really knowing what we are doing. I am teaching a course on innovative entrepreneurship, but I am doing so utterly without evidence as to the topics that should be emphasized, [or] the tools the students should learn to utilize. My state of mind on these matters is like that of 18th-century physicians, who used leeches and cupping to treat their patients simply because previous physicians had done so."[12]

In an effort to fill part of this knowledge gap as it pertains to online learning, the ITHAKA organization mounted an empirical study of the learning outcomes associated with the use of a prototype statistics course developed by Carnegie Mellon University, taught in hybrid mode (with one face-to-face Q&A session a week).[13] Carnegie Mellon's course has several appealing features, including its use of cognitive tutors and feedback loops to guide students through instruction in basic concepts.[14] In our study, we used a randomized trials approach, involving more than six hundred participants across six public university campuses, to compare the learning outcomes of students who took a hybrid-online version of this highly interactive course with the outcomes of students who took face-to-face counterpart courses. A rich array of data was collected at the State University of New York (SUNY), the City University of New York (CUNY), and the University System of Maryland. Although this study had limitations of its own, it is, we believe, the most rigorous assessment to date of the use of a sophisticated online course by the kinds of public universities that most desperately need to counteract the cost disease.[15] I will cite only two principal findings about learning outcomes.

First, we found *no statistically significant differences in standard measures of learning outcomes* (pass or completion rates, scores on common final exam questions, and results of a national test of statistical literacy) between students in the traditional classes and students in the hybrid-online format classes (see figure 4).[16] This finding, in and of itself, is not different from the results of many other studies. But it is important to emphasize that the relevant effect coefficients in this study have very small standard errors. One commentator, Michael S. McPherson, president of the Spencer Foundation, observed

**Figure 4** Effect of hybrid format on student learning outcomes

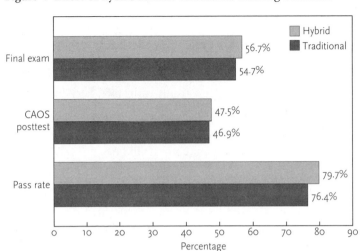

*Note:* None of the differences between traditional and hybrid courses was statistically significant at the 10 percent level.

that what we have here are "quite precisely estimated zeros." That is, if there had in fact been pronounced differences in outcomes between traditional-format and hybrid-format groups, it is highly likely that we would have found them.[17]

Second, this finding is *consistent not only across campuses, but also across subgroups of what was a very diverse student population.* Half the students in our study came from families with incomes of less than $50,000, and half were first-generation college students. Fewer than half were white, and the group was about evenly divided between students with college GPAs above and below 3.0. The finding of consistent outcomes across this varied population rebuts the proposition that only exceptionally well-prepared, high-achieving students can succeed in online settings.[18]

Thus, while we did not find transformational improvements in learning outcomes, we did obtain compelling evidence that students with a wide range of characteristics learned just as much in the hybrid-online format as they would have had they instead taken the course in the traditional format.[19] Students at the four-year universities in our study paid no price for taking a hybrid course in terms of pass rates or other learning outcomes. This seemingly bland result is, in fact, very important, in light of perhaps the most common reason given by faculty and deans for resisting the use of online instruction: "We worry that basic student learning outcomes will be hurt, and we won't expose our students to this risk." The ITHAKA research suggests that such worries may not be well founded—at least in situations akin to those we studied.

Several commentators on our study have expressed the hope—bordering on a conviction—that improvements in both the online offerings themselves and in the skill with which they are taught will lead, perhaps before long, to even better learning outcomes for such online offerings. The pace of change is dizzying, and improvements in pedagogy are almost certain to be made. In this regard, the pioneering work of the Khan Academy should be acknowledged. Salman Khan and his colleagues continue to learn a great deal about the most effective ways of using the online medium to teach.[20] More generally, institutions and their faculty are likely to become increasingly adept at using the feedback and other features of sophisticated online courses. Thus, there is, I agree, reason to believe that the findings we have reported for learning outcomes are a kind of baseline. Future studies may well obtain evidence that is even more favorable to continued experimentation with online approaches. But that is in the future and is simply another reason for advocating both continued development of these pedagogies and rigorous testing of their effectiveness.

What about cost savings? Whether pedagogies such as the one we tested can in fact reduce instructional costs, thereby lowering the denominator of the productivity ratio, is an absolutely central question—which is given even more prominence by our finding of equivalent learning outcomes at even this early stage in the development of sophisticated online systems. Because of its clear importance, we thought hard about how to estimate potential cost savings. But, truth be told, we did not do nearly as well in looking at the "cost" blade of the scissors as we did in looking at learning outcomes. We were able to do no more than suggest a method of approach and hazard what are little more than rough guesses (speculations) as to the conceivable magnitude of potential savings in staffing costs.

A fundamental problem, cutting across all types of online offerings, is that contemporaneous comparisons of the costs of traditional modes of teaching and of newly instituted online pedagogies are nearly useless in projecting steady-state savings—or, worse yet, highly misleading. The reason is that the costs of doing almost anything for the first time are very different from the costs of doing the same thing numerous times. That admonition is especially true in the case of online learning. There are substantial start-up costs associated with course development that have to be considered in the short run but that are likely to decrease over time, as well as transition costs involved in moving from the traditional, mostly face-to-face, model to a hybrid model of the kind that we studied. Instructors need to be trained to take full advantage of automated systems with feedback loops. Also, there may well be contractual limits on section size that were designed with the traditional model in mind but that do not make sense for a hybrid model. Such constraints have to be accepted in the short term, even though it may be possible to modify them over time.[21]

To overcome (avoid!) these problems, we carried out simulated cost probes. We conceptualized the research question not as "How much will institutions save right now by shifting to hybrid learning?" but rather as "Under what assumptions will cost savings be realized, over time, by shifting to a hybrid format, and how large are those savings likely to be?"

The crude models we employed (which ignore entirely the "joint products" issue that grows out of the practice of supporting graduate students as teaching assistants) suggest savings in compensation costs alone ranging from 36 percent to 57 percent when the traditional teaching mode relies on multiple sections.[22] Of course, this simulation underestimates substantially the potential savings from moving toward a hybrid model because it does not account for space costs, which, in many instances, can dominate cost calculations. A fuller analysis would also deal with other infrastructure costs, some of which would undoubtedly be higher in a hybrid format, as well as take into account reductions in the time costs incurred by students.[23]

Also highly relevant are the potentially profound effects of simplifications in scheduling and easier acceptance of transfer credits and evidence of prior learning. These could well lead, for many students, to an accelerated flow through the system, and thus to reduced time-to-degree and higher completion rates. If more students can be educated and if time-to-degree can be reduced, all without commensurate increases in costs, productivity could increase substantially via this avenue of impact.[24] Careful modeling of new scheduling possibilities, and of the implications for time-to-degree and completion rates, is definitely in order.

ITHAKA's empirical study is undoubtedly helpful in overcoming skepticism about the learning outcomes of online offerings, but we must remember that it involved only one course, in a field well suited to online learning, in predominantly onsite contexts. We need many more careful studies of varied approaches to online learning, carried out in a variety of settings (including two-year colleges as well as a variety of four-year institutions). It is encouraging that the MOOC provider edX, with support from the Bill & Melinda Gates Foundation, is collaborating with two Boston-area community colleges to introduce an adapted version of an MIT online course in computer science (in what sounds like a hybrid mode).[25] It will be interesting to see how successfully this MIT offering can be adapted to the needs of quite different student populations. Careful assessment of learning outcomes, preferably by a third party, would be instructive.

Nor is it sufficient simply to compare outcomes of particular online offerings with outcomes in traditional face-to-face courses. We also need studies that compare the effectiveness of different approaches to online learning. We elected to test the Carnegie Mellon course because we believed that the highly interactive character of the CMU course, informed by cognitive science, was more promising than simpler approaches. But this course was expensive to develop.[26] Its value needs to be compared with the value of other approaches that are cheaper and less complex. It would also be highly desirable to compare outcomes and costs associated with various MOOCs against other approaches to online teaching. And we have to recognize that the answers to these questions about the costs and benefits of different approaches are likely to vary according to the content being presented, the student population, and the setting. ITHAKA, working with the MOOC provider Coursera and others, is engaged in just such a cross-platform study in collaboration with the University System of Maryland.[27]

Designing research strategies in this area is a complicated business under the best of circumstances. Randomized trials are, it is generally agreed, the most promising way of reducing the ever-present risk of selection bias, but a huge takeaway from our empirical research using this methodology is that it is expensive and devilishly difficult to carry out. As we learned painfully, there are many important details that have to be worked out: how best to describe the course to be tested, how to recruit student participants in the study (including what incentives to use), how to randomize apprehensive students between "treatment" and "control" groups (and how to be sure that they stay in their assigned group), how to collect background information about student participants, and how to satisfy institutional review board (IRB) requirements in a timely way. Moreover, finding good answers requires the day-to-day involvement of campus staff not directly responsible to outsiders like us.[28] Looking ahead, I now think—heresy of heresies!—that the case for using randomized trials should itself be subject to careful cost-benefit analysis.[29] Appealing as they are, this may be an instance in which, in at least some cases, "the best is the enemy of the good."[30]

Last on my short list of research priorities is the evident need for creative analyses on the cost side of the ledger. This work should do more than just project direct costs (on a forward-looking, steady-state basis). It should include an analysis of implications for space utilization, capital costs, and indirect costs, hard as these are to estimate. It should also consider freshly the many ways in which online technologies may influence the way sizeable parts of the curriculum can be re-engineered (bearing in mind the injunction of the authors of the *New England Journal of Medicine* article about the need for such re-engineering, as in the much earlier introduction of electricity to manufacturing).[31] The pace at which current students get through the educational system is enormously important, as are completion rates. It may be possible to utilize online technologies to allow energetic secondary school students to get an early start on their college education— perhaps by preparing them to take college-level tests that will allow them to place out of some introductory courses. Alternatively, given that the out-of-pocket costs of enrollment, and of attrition, are relatively low compared to the costs of traditional courses for which students need to pay tuition, MOOCs could allow students to experiment with different classes and get a sense of what disciplines interest them before they ever set foot on campus.[32]

The biggest opportunity for MOOCs to raise productivity system-wide, and to lower costs, may well lie in finding effective ways for third parties to certify the "credit-worthiness" of their courses—and the success of students in passing them. The American Council on Education and Coursera have announced a pilot project that will entail faculty-led assessments of a subset of Coursera offerings. Students who complete courses that satisfy the requirements of the ACE's standard College Credit Recommendation Service, and who pass an identity-verified exam, will be able to have a transcript submitted to the college of their choice. It will then be up to individual colleges to decide whether to give transfer credit for such work, though at present more than two thousand colleges and universities across the country generally accept ACE credit recommendations.[33] One key question to be addressed by colleges contemplating accepting such credentials will be how to define the coherence of the totality of the coursework that they expect students to complete in order to receive one of their degrees.

### The Need for Customizable, Sustainable Platforms (or Tool Kits)

I now move on to discuss another type of need if we are to make real progress in utilizing technology in the pursuit of our aspirations. A major conclusion of ITHAKA's *Barriers to Adoption* report is that "perhaps the largest obstacle to widespread adoption of ILO [interactive learning online]–style courses" is the lack at the present time of a "sustainable platform that allows interested faculty either to create a fully interactive, machine-guided learning environment, or to customize a course that has been created by someone else (and thus claim it as their own)." A companion conclusion is that "faculty are extremely reluctant to teach courses that they do not 'own.'"[34] As one commentator cited in the *Barriers* report put it, "No one wants to give someone else's speech" (even though all of us are happy to borrow felicitous phrases). This is by no means just about ego, although ego is certainly involved. Faculty may understandably feel that they are not sufficiently familiar with content prepared solely by someone else to teach it effectively. Also, both the structure of content and examples often need to be tailored to a particular student audience.[35]

It would be easy—but incorrect—to infer from this line of argument, which emphasizes the need for customization, that the development of online courses has to be a responsibility of each individual campus. Sole reliance on purely homegrown approaches would be foolishly inefficient and simply would not work in most settings. It would not take advantage of the economies of scale offered by sophisticated software that incorporates features of well-developed platforms, including elaborate feedback loops and instructive peer-to-peer interactions.[36] Furthermore, many institutions simply do not have the money or the in-house talent to start from scratch in creating sophisticated online learning systems that can be disseminated widely. Nor would it make sense to re-invent wheels that can be readily shared.

*There is clearly a system-wide need for sophisticated, customizable platforms (or tool kits) that can be made widely available, maintained, upgraded, and sustained in a cost-effective manner.* Yet higher education thus far has failed to find a convincing solution to this problem, and immediate prospects for a solution are uncertain at best. In seeking to address this need, we must recognize the high probability that quite different pedagogies—and therefore somewhat different platforms—will be appropriate in subjects in which there are concrete concepts to be mastered and one right answer to many questions (for example, basic statistics)—as contrasted with discursive subjects which benefit from the exchange of different points of view (e.g., the Arab-Israeli conflict). At one point, I was much more inclined than I am at present to believe that a single platform or single tool kit might be appropriate. It now seems clear to me that the notion of a single dominant platform is unrealistic, given the entrepreneurial inclinations of numerous individuals and organizations. I now believe that such a notion is also unwise. There is much to be said for experimentation with different models and for competition among models as we search for approaches well suited to different needs. Adoption of any specific platform or platforms should be driven by a compelling strategy.

How should such platforms be developed? A strong prima facie case can be made for a high-level, collaborative effort within the traditional higher education community; after all, collaborations have been highly beneficial in sharing other assets, such as ultra-expensive scientific equipment. It is, however, widely recognized that collaborative efforts are difficult to organize, especially when much nimbleness is needed.[37] Collective decision-making is often cumbersome, and it can be hard to avoid lowest-common-denominator thinking. My favorite example is the Peace of Paris negotiations at the end of World War I, which ended so disastrously. John Maynard Keynes's famous account of the collective efforts of the participants is worth recalling: "These then were the personalities of Paris—I forbear to mention other nations or lesser men: Clemenceau, aesthetically the noblest; the President, morally the most admirable; Lloyd George, intellectually the subtlest. Out of their disparities and weaknesses the Treaty was born, child of the least worthy attributes of each of its parents, without nobility, without morality, without intellect."[38]

There is, then, much to be said for seeking leadership from individual entities that are well-respected and have demonstrated a capacity to *execute*. Early on in our thinking about this issue, my colleagues and I were wondering whether Carnegie Mellon might address this need by scaling up the promising, highly interactive system that we tested and correcting the main shortcomings noted by participants in our study, including their interest in having a more customizable platform. Carnegie Mellon has expressed a commitment to developing the tools that are needed for authoring and analytics, which could well improve the scalability of their platform as we had originally hoped, but such an outcome is likely to be at least a year away.[39] In a field that is evolving as rapidly as this one, it remains to be seen how CMU's cognitive-science, adaptive-learning approach will fit into the online learning landscape over the next few years.

We could, of course, simply let the marketplace provide: it is possible that for-profit entities, trading on financial incentives, might develop one or more effective platforms. There is, however, a risk that a for-profit might elect to cover some or all of its costs by essentially privatizing the significant amounts of information that such online systems can generate about how students learn. The example of Google illustrates dramatically the value that can be derived from exploiting a proprietary database for purposes such as selling targeted advertising. Massive amounts of data on how students learn can further the core mission of not-for-profit higher education and lead, in time, to the creation of better adaptive-learning systems. It would be unfortunate if the potential "public good" benefits of the rich information generated by online learning systems were lost. The educational community writ large should think hard about whether, and if so how, a depository for such information could be created and maintained. Such a depository should probably be created under the auspices of a nonprofit entity that recognizes explicitly the value of broad access to such critically important data. We should not think, however, that nonprofits are immune from the temptation to privatize and control data. There are too many examples, in publishing and in other fields, of situations in which nonprofits act very much like their for-profit cousins.

I have left for last what I regard as the most promising (though still entirely speculative) option at present: namely, the possibility that leading MOOCs might meet the need for readily adaptable platforms or tool kits. The developers of Coursera, edX, and Stanford's Class2Go platform have said that they are committed to developing systems that can be used widely by others.[40] No one should doubt the good intentions of such entities. Nor should anyone undervalue the substantial resources at their disposal. It is precisely because they have a rare combination of assets—impressive technical capacity, a strong financial base, and real standing in the academic community (enhanced by extraordinary media coverage)—that I regard them, at least right now, as the highest-potential game in town. But neither should anyone underestimate the difficulty of modifying MOOCs originally designed to provide direct instruction to many thousands of individual students worldwide so that they can also serve the needs of existing educational institutions that serve defined student populations.[41]

The interviews we did for our *Barriers* study revealed "little enthusiasm for prepackaged online courses that did not permit customization, regardless of the institution 'sponsoring' the course, its quality, or the degree of interactivity."[42] And there is something of an inherent conflict, or at least a tension, between, on the one hand, the structure of MOOC offerings, which are designed largely by renowned and high-visibility professors at leading universities and which are generally provided worldwide on an "as-is" basis and, on the other hand, the need for at least some campus-specific customization. A related point is that the cost-effectiveness of MOOCs in their "direct to student" mode stems largely from the fact that their one-size-fits-all structure drives the marginal cost of serving even an extra

thousand students close to zero. It is much less obvious how—
or even whether—large cost savings can be achieved when a
MOOC has to be customized for local use by a particular institution with a much smaller student population and a resident
teaching staff. In addition, there are complex intellectual property rights issues that need to be resolved.[43]

We should also recognize that while there has been much
discussion about potential sources of revenue for MOOCs
(charging for certificates of completion, becoming a kind of
job-placement enterprise, and so on), the viability of the various hypothetical possibilities remains to be demonstrated.[44] A
major lesson from the earlier MIT OpenCourseWare (OCW)
experience is that it can be much easier to create something like
OCW, often with philanthropic support, than to find regular
sources of revenue to pay the ongoing costs of maintaining and
upgrading the system. MIT is today still paying the running
costs of OCW each year, and we are told that the faculty and
trustees of MIT are convinced that they cannot go down the
same path again—their pride in OCW as a truly pioneering
venture notwithstanding.[45] Donor fatigue is a fact of life, and
some regular, predictable source of revenue is needed for sustainability. There is real danger in announcing that something
is free without knowing who is to pay the ongoing costs, which
are all too real and cannot be ignored.[46] The "no free lunch"
adage comes to mind.

These cautions and open questions about MOOCs cannot
be ignored or assumed away. Nonetheless, I believe that the
educational community should make every effort to take
advantage of the great strengths of the leading MOOCs. Not
only should we encourage their continuing interest in serving
existing institutions as well as a global audience of individuals,
but we should also try to find ways of testing learning outcomes and assessing cost-saving options for specific universities
and university systems. It seems clear that MOOCs have an

extraordinary capacity to improve access to educational materials from renowned instructors in various subjects for learners throughout the world. However, as far as I am aware, right now there is no compelling evidence as to how well MOOCs can produce good learning outcomes for 18- to 22-year-olds of various backgrounds studying on mainline campuses—and this is an enormous gap in our knowledge.

There is good reason to be extremely cautious in extrapolating crude findings for the student population that took the first MOOCs to mainline student populations. A highly preliminary study of the demographics of a MOOC in circuits and electronics, which at the time was offered by MITx but which is now offered by the larger edX organization, found that those students still around at the end of the course bore almost no resemblance to the students on mainline campuses in this country. One dramatic statistic: four out of five students who completed that MOOC had taken a comparable course at a traditional university prior to working their way through the MITx course. The circuits and electronics MOOC completers also differed along many other dimensions from traditional on-campus populations.[47]

In addition to pursuing aggressively these key questions concerning learning outcomes on mainline campuses, the entire higher education community has an interest in thinking about business models that would assure the sustainability of the most promising MOOCs without compromising educational goals.[48] The experiences of entities such as JSTOR in developing sustainable business models could be relevant. Indeed, I suspect that at least part of the answer to the sustainability issue could lie in finding a JSTOR-like mechanism for charging reasonable fees to institutions (and/or students) that realize cost-saving benefits from MOOCs. Coursera and Antioch University have reached a content-licensing agreement that seems to move at least some distance in this direction.[49]

## The Need for New Mindsets—and
## Fresh Thinking about Decision-Making

My last category of challenges to be addressed is something of a grab bag—but a useful one, I hope. Many of the specific issues mentioned in the *Barriers* report share the attribute of requiring strong institutional leadership and even fresh ways of thinking about decision-making. These include, for example, the fact that "online instruction is alien to most faculty and calls into question the very reason that many pursued an academic career in the first place. . . . they had enjoyed being students, and valued the relationships that they enjoyed with their professors."[50] Other barriers include the fear that online instruction will be used to diminish faculty ranks and the failure to provide the right incentives for faculty who are asked to lead online initiatives.

Hard as it sometimes is for beleaguered deans and presidents to confront challenges of these kinds directly, it is rarely wise to gloss over the most sensitive issues. I am convinced that a new, tougher, mindset is a prerequisite to progress. There is too strong a tendency to respond to financial pressures by economizing around the edges and putting off bigger—and harder—choices in the hope that the sun will shine tomorrow (even if the forecast is for rain!).

The seemingly unrelenting upward spiral of costs and tuition charges can be arrested, at least in some degree, only if presidents, provosts, and trustees make controlling both costs and tuition increases a priority. Academic leaders must look explicitly for strategies to lower costs. I am not saying that educational leaders lack courage (though, sadly, some do). The reality is that controlling costs is a hard sell, in part because strong forces are pushing in the opposite direction. As one of our advisers said, "Those opposed have so many ways of throwing sand in the wheels."[51]

I continue to believe that the potential for online learning to help reduce costs without adversely affecting educational outcomes is very real. Absent strong leadership, however, there is a high probability that any productivity gains from online education will be used to gild the educational/research lily—as has been the norm for the last twenty years. Presidents and provosts should not mince words in charging their deans and faculty with teaching courses of comparable or superior quality with fewer resources—thereby either lowering the denominator of the productivity ratio or raising the student-learning component of the numerator (or both).[52]

There is a definite political aspect to all of this. *We must recognize that if higher education does not begin to slow the rate of increase in college costs, our nation's higher education system will lose the public support on which it so heavily depends.* There has been an undeniable erosion of public trust in the capacity of higher education to operate more efficiently.[53] In this respect, the better-off private and public universities—which rely heavily on many forms of federal support, including direct research grants from the National Institutes of Health, National Science Foundation, and other federal agencies; indirect cost recovery; financing of graduate students; and student loan guarantees—are in much the same boat as the more obviously endangered parts of the educational system. Efforts to save resources should be highly visible. Those who are skeptical about the capacity of established institutions to take positive steps in this sensitive area need to be given evidence that change is possible.

One favorable omen is the openness of many faculty to new ways of thinking—including the desirability of "flipping the classroom."[54] A recent survey shows that a "decisive majority of professors"—69 percent—view with more excitement than fear the prospect of "changing the faculty role to spend less time lecturing and more time coaching students."[55] Movement away from reliance on traditional lecturing, especially in large introductory courses, should allow institutions to devote the valuable in-person time of both faculty and students to activities that are more powerfully educational. Flipping the classroom need not save resources, however, and can even lead to higher costs. Lecturing is highly cost-efficient, whatever its educational shortcomings. Institutions that decide to flip the classroom should be well aware of this fact and should see if there are ways of saving resources by reducing the total amount of time spent in small group sessions (while, one would hope, improving the quality of the time that is spent). The hybrid version of the Carnegie Mellon statistics course that we tested is one possible model.

Growing openness to such concepts does not translate automatically, however, into new modes of teaching. Required is a willingness to question established norms, including models of decision-making. The challenges are at least as much conceptual, organizational, and administrative as they are technical. I wonder if the particular models of what is often called "shared governance" that have been developed over the last century are well suited to the digital world. Shared governance can mean dividing up tasks in seemingly clear-cut ways: leaving "corporate" decisions of one kind or another entirely in the hands of trustees and "academic" decisions entirely in the hands of faculty.[56] But if wise decisions are to be made in key areas, such as teaching methods, it is imperative that they be made by a mix of individuals from different parts of the institution—including faculty leaders but also others well-positioned to consider the full ramifications of the choices before them. There are real dangers in relying on the compartmentalized thinking that too often accompanies decentralized modes of organization to which we have become accustomed.[57]

Given the institution-wide stakes associated with judgments as to when and how digital technologies should be used to teach some kinds of content, there is a strong case to be made for genuinely collaborative decision-making that includes faculty, of course, but that does not give full authority to determine teaching methods to particular professors or even to particular departments. There are too many spillover effects. It is by no means obvious that resources saved by using machine-guided learning in large introductory courses in subjects especially well suited to this approach should be captured in their entirety by the departments concerned.[58] It is important to think in terms of the institution as a whole in allocating savings—with prospective students and their parents among the stakeholders who deserve consideration. Also, the investments required to allow such savings—and to sustain initiatives—can be considerable and often have to be approved by a central authority.

Specific organizational solutions will vary from institution to institution, but the general principle is clear: some centralized calibration of both benefits and costs is essential. In a less complex age, it may have been sensible to leave almost all decisions concerning not just what to teach but *how* to teach in the hands of individual faculty members. It is by no means clear, however, that this model is the right one going forward, and it would be highly desirable if the academic community were seized of this issue and addressed it before "outsiders" dictate their own solutions. To repeat: faculty involvement is essential. There is a self-evident need for consultation with those who are expert in their disciplines and experienced in teaching—but this is not the same thing as giving faculty veto power over change.

Nor is this, I would emphasize, an issue of academic freedom, as that crucially important concept is properly understood. Faculty members should certainly be entirely free to speak their minds, as scholars and as teachers. But this freedom of expression should not imply unilateral control over methods of teaching. There is nothing in the basic documents explaining academic freedom to suggest that such control is included. It is not.[59] If academic freedom is construed to mean that faculty can do anything they choose, it becomes both meaningless and indefensible.[60]

The case for genuinely fresh thinking about decision-making and shared governance rests only in part on the need for institutions to make carefully considered decisions about teaching methods in specific situations. It is also based on the fundamental nature of digital technologies, and the changes in the storage and dissemination of information, that are everywhere evident. One does not have to believe—as I certainly do not—that methods of online teaching, including MOOCs, will lead to diminished interest in high-quality residential education to recognize that the broader structure of higher education is likely to change quite profoundly. What we are witnessing is the early stage of at least a partial unbundling of activities that used to be the responsibility of a single faculty member or of groups of faculty in a single campus location: creating knowledge, teaching content, testing students' grasp of that content, and credentialing.[61] Joseph Aoun, president of Northeastern University, describes this as a "vertically integrated model," and he contrasts it with the rise of "horizontal" models in which different people may perform some of these core functions—and perform them in different locations and for much larger numbers of students.[62]

In the more horizontal model that Aoun and others envision, the roles of some faculty may be quite different than they are today. Different mixes of talents and inclinations will be required, and the organizational and administrative questions will be challenging. Some people and some institutions will undoubtedly resist such changes—some wisely, some unwisely. The New York University professor and writer Clay Shirky compares what is going on in some parts of education today with what happened to the recording industry when large numbers of people started to listen to MP3s. He describes this pattern as "a new story rearranging people's sense of the possible, with the incumbents the last to know. . . . First, the people running the old system don't notice the change. When they do, they assume it's minor. Then that it's a niche. Then a fad. And by the time they understand that the world has actually changed, they've squandered most of the time that they had to adapt."[63]

No one can say confidently how powerful or how pervasive the horizontal model will turn out to be—how many colleges and universities will be affected, and in what ways. But it seems clear that all of us interested in the future of colleges and universities, and in preserving key roles for faculty, are well advised to do our best to get some distance "ahead of the wave" (to return to John Hennessy's tsunami metaphor).[64] It is an open question how the structure of decision-making and the definition of shared governance need to be modified in light of these changes brought on by the still rapidly evolving Internet age.[65] And it is a question that those of us in the academy, or with close ties to it, should be pondering now, before more time elapses.

## What Must We Retain?

Let me now circle back to what I said earlier. As we contemplate a rapidly evolving world in which greater and greater use will surely be made of online modes of teaching, I am convinced that there are central aspects of life on our traditional campuses that must not only be retained but even strengthened. I will mention three.

First is the need to emphasize—and, if need be, to re-emphasize—the great value of "minds rubbing against minds." We should resist efforts to overdo online instruction, important as it can be. There are, of course, both economic constraints and practical limitations on how much education can be delivered in person. But those of us who have benefited from personal interactions with brilliant teachers (some of whom became close friends), as I certainly have, can testify to the inspirational, life-changing aspects of such experiences. The half-life of content taught in a course can be short, as we all know; but great teachers change the way their students see the world (and themselves) long after the students have forgotten formulas, theorems, and even engaging illustrations of this or that proposition.[66] Moreover, a great advantage of residential institutions is that genuine learning occurs more or less continually, and as often, or more often, out of the classroom as in it. This cliché, repeated by countless presidents and deans, conveys real truth. Late-night peer-to-peer exchanges offer students hard-to-replicate access to the perspectives of other people. As one of my greatest teachers, Jacob Viner, never tired of warning his students, "There is no limit to the amount of nonsense you can think, if you think too long alone."

My plea is for the adoption of a portfolio approach to curricular development that provides a carefully calibrated mix of instructional styles. This mix will vary by institutional type, and relatively wealthy liberal arts colleges and selective universities can be expected to offer more in-person teaching than can many less privileged institutions. However, even the wealthiest, most elite colleges and universities that seemingly can afford to stay pretty much as they are, at least in the short run, should ask if failing to participate in the evolution of online learning models is to their advantage, or even realistic, in the long run.[67] Their students, along with others of their generation, will expect to use digital resources—and to be trained in their use. And as technologies grow increasingly sophisticated, and we learn more about how students learn and what pedagogical methods work best in various fields, even top-tier institutions will stand to gain from the use of such technologies to improve student learning.

Second, we must retain, whatever the provocations, the unswerving commitment of great colleges and universities to freedom of thought—as exemplified so clearly by my great friend of so many years, Richard Lyman, Stanford's seventh president, who died in May of this year. President Lyman stood resolutely for civility and protection of the rights of all. When he was compelled to summon the police to curb an over-the-edge demonstration in 1969, his action was applauded by some, but he thought the applause was misplaced. President Lyman said: "Anytime it becomes necessary for a university to summon the police, a defeat has taken place. The victory we seek at Stanford is not like a military victory; it is a victory of reason and the examined life over unreason and the tyranny of coercion."[68]

Third, our colleges and universities should focus unashamedly on values as well as on knowledge—and we should spend more time than we usually do considering how best to do this.[69] This is most definitely not a plea for pontificating. When President Robert Hutchins was urged to teach his students at Chicago to do this, that, or the other thing, he demurred, explaining: "All attempts to teach character directly will fail. They degenerate into vague exhortations to be good which leave the bored listener with a desire to commit outrages which would otherwise have never occurred to him."[70]

Let me now refer to a baccalaureate address given at Princeton in 2010 by Jeff Bezos, the CEO of Amazon, titled "We Are What We Choose."[71] Bezos began by reciting a poignant story of a trip he took with his grandparents when he was ten years old. While riding in their Airstream trailer, this precocious ten-year old laboriously calculated the damage to her health that his grandmother was doing by smoking. His conclusion was that, at two minutes per puff, she was taking nine years off her life. When he proudly told her of his finding, she burst into tears. His grandfather stopped the car and gently said to the young Bezos: "One day you'll understand that it's harder to be kind than clever." Bezos went on in his address to talk about the difference between gifts and choices. "Cleverness," he said, "is a gift, kindness is a choice. Gifts are easy—they're given, after all. Choices can be hard." Colleges and universities can, and should, find ways to help their students learn this key distinction—and encourage them, at least some of the time, to choose kindness over cleverness.

I return, finally (which one of my friends called the most beautiful word in the English language), to the question posed at the outset of this book: is online learning a fix for the cost disease? My answer: no, not by itself. But it can be part of an answer. It is certainly no panacea for this country's deep-seated educational problems, which are rooted in social issues, fiscal dilemmas, and national priorities, as well as historical practices. In the case of a topic as active as online learning, we should expect inflated claims of spectacular successes—and of blatant failures. The findings I have reported warn strongly against too much hype. What Kin Hubbard famously said about those who claim certain knowledge of the currency question can be applied to online learning: "Only one fellow in ten thousand understands the currency question, and we meet him every day." There is a real danger that the media frenzy associated with MOOCs will lead some colleges and universities (and, especially, business-oriented members of their boards) to embrace too tightly the MOOC approach before it is adequately tested and found to be both sustainable and capable of delivering good learning outcomes for all kinds of students.[72]

Uncertainties notwithstanding, it is clear to me that online systems have great potential. Vigorous efforts should be made to explore further uses of both the relatively simple systems that are proliferating all around us, often to good effect, and more sophisticated systems that are still in their infancy—systems sure to improve over time, perhaps dramatically. In these explorations, I would urge us not to hesitate to experiment, but always to insist on assessments of outcomes. I would also urge us to think in terms of system-wide approaches and to exercise that rarest of virtues, patience. The careful development (and testing) of promising new pedagogies can take years and even decades.[73]

I will end with a last story, on this theme of patience. It comes from the Arabian Nights, and I owe it to a very wise man, Ezra Zilkha, who was born in Baghdad. This is the story of the black horse. A prisoner who was about to be executed was having his last audience with the sultan. He implored the sultan: "If you will spare me for one year, I will teach your favorite black horse to talk." The sultan agreed immediately with this request, and the prisoner was returned to his quarters. When his fellow prisoners heard what had happened, they mocked him: "How can you possibly teach a horse to talk? Absurd." He replied: "Wait a minute. Think. A year is a long time. In a year, I could die naturally, the sultan could die, the horse could die, or, who knows, I might teach the black horse to talk." The lesson of the story, Mr. Zilkha said, is, "If you don't have an immediate answer, buy time. Time, if we use it, might make us adapt and maybe, who knows, find solutions." If speaking to a college or university audience such as this one, Mr. Zilkha would add: "It is the job of the Stanfords of this world to teach the black horse to talk."

## APPENDIX: THE ONLINE LEARNING LANDSCAPE

### Contours

At one end of this highly variegated landscape is an extremely large number of relatively straightforward online courses that provide an assortment of instructional materials on the web, often including videos, practice problems, and homework assignments. These courses (and some entire degree programs based on them) are usually institution-specific and built on learning management systems; they can be aimed at students in residence, distance learning populations, or both. They usually carry credit and are offered by both for-profit universities such as the University of Phoenix and a wide variety of nonprofit educational institutions. Some such courses in the nonprofit sector—not all of them entirely or even mostly online—have been created with the assistance of the National Center for Academic Transformation (NCAT) through its course-redesign initiative, which itself involves different models of online instruction.[74]

According to a January 2013 report by the Babson Survey Research Group, the Sloan Consortium, and Pearson, about one in three college students now takes at least one online course (compared with about one in ten in fall 2002, the first year the survey was administered), and whereas total enrollments in higher education declined between fall 2010 and fall 2011, online enrollments grew about 9 percent during that time period.[75] Indeed, the current spread of online offerings is dizzying. During one week in August 2012, I came across announcements of online initiatives by the University of Florida system, a Seminole tribe program also in Florida (the Native Learning Center), University of Kansas, Utah Valley University, and a number of HBCUs whose activities were reported by the Digital Learning Lab of Howard University. (Websites are the best way to learn about these, and other initiatives too numerous even to mention here.) In addition, there are many online courses overseas, and the Open University in the United Kingdom has been especially active in this field for years.[76] In September 2012, Indiana University announced IU Online, a major new initiative that builds on a long history of work at that university and illustrates what is happening at a variety of institutions throughout the country.[77]

The proliferation of offerings called *online* surely qualifies as a tidal wave, if not yet a tsunami. In addition to courses that can be counted, all of us feel the pervasiveness of the Internet in higher education by the increasing use of it in standard course-management systems, virtual reading materials, and a rapidly proliferating number of more and more sophisticated electronic textbooks incorporated into the curriculum. Even courses that are called "traditional" almost always involve some use of digital resources.

Carnegie Mellon University deserves special mention as a pioneer in the development of highly interactive online courses that have been built by teams of cognitive scientists, software engineers, and disciplinary specialists under the leadership of Candace Thille's Open Learning Initiative. These OLI courses feature cognitive tutors—which draw on principles from cognitive psychology to guide a student through learning activities, taking into account the student's progress—and three types of feedback loops: system to student, providing instant feedback to students on their answers to problems and carefully structured hints as to how to get the right answers; system to teacher, providing current information to the teacher on how individual students, as well as students in general, are doing (thereby enabling teachers to make more effective use of any face-to-face time that is available); and system to course designer, providing information on parts of the course that are working well and parts that need improvement.[78]

At still another corner of this landscape are the MOOCs (massive open online courses)—usually designed by highly regarded professionals and taught to thousands of students worldwide by well-known professors. Typically, students who have registered for these courses (usually for free) watch videos and complete assignments that are machine-graded or graded by other students and/or teaching assistants. With very few exceptions, these courses do not carry college credit or lead to degrees, and they may or may not lead to certificates of accomplishment or badges (for which students may need to pay a modest fee) that indicate mastery of particular skills. Three of the best-known exemplars of MOOCs are listed below:

- Coursera, a for-profit spin-off from Stanford that offers a wide variety of courses in close collaboration with several dozen high-profile universities (including Princeton, the University of Toronto, and the University of Michigan, as well as Stanford), to which Coursera provides authoring tools and other forms of assistance;
- Udacity, another for-profit Stanford spin-off, which concentrates on computer science and related fields; unlike Coursera, Udacity works only with individual professors (rather than through institutions);
- edX, a nonprofit partnership of MIT, Harvard, the University of California at Berkeley, Georgetown, Wellesley, and the University of Texas System that offers courses of its own, initially focusing mainly on computer science and engineering, and which also plans to make its platform available on an open-source basis to faculty elsewhere who wish to create their own courses.[79]

Again, websites are the best source of information about these and other MOOCs.

Another well-known provider of free online course materials is Khan Academy, a nonprofit organization which is perhaps best known for its short instructional videos hosted on YouTube, but which today emphasizes automated practice exercises that are used heavily by secondary school students. Its instructional videos cover a broad range of disciplines, ranging from civics and art history to computer science, chemistry, differential equations, and the Greek debt crisis, though it has generally been Khan's mathematics materials that are used in classroom settings. While one can argue about whether Khan Academy should be classified as a MOOC, in light of the fact that its typical offerings are not courses, the breadth and widespread appeal of the Khan Academy's offerings undoubtedly bear mention.

In mid-November 2012, a consortium of ten prominent universities announced that it will offer credit-bearing online courses, starting in fall 2013, as part of an initiative called Semester Online.[80] The consortium will operate through the platform developed by the educational technology company 2U. Both students enrolled in the member institutions and students outside those institutions will be able to take the thirty or so courses offered by the consortium members for credit, though students outside the host universities will have to apply to take the courses and, if admitted, pay tuition for those courses. Unlike MOOC providers, this consortium will emphasize small, live "virtual" discussion groups in which students interact with each other and with the instructor in real time. The small class sizes and synchronous nature of the interactions are likely to make these offerings more expensive than MOOCs and some other online courses.

### Distinctions

In contemplating the wide array of offerings that populate the online universe, it may be helpful to think in terms of eleven overlapping distinctions, grouped under four headings.

## Particular Features of Online Courses

1. How advanced is the content of the course, and are there daunting prerequisites?

2. To what extent does the course contain cognitive tutors (akin to those available in Carnegie Mellon's OLI courses) or other adaptive learning features?

3. To what extent does the course allow learners to interact with each other, and perhaps with instructors or teaching assistants who are leading or overseeing the course (if there are any)?

## How Content Is Delivered

4. Is the course purely online, or is it a hybrid course with a face-to-face element?

5. Is the online component of the course offered in synchronous mode (that is, do students all have to be online at the same, specified times), or in asynchronous mode (where students can access the materials any time they choose), or both?

## Entities Offering the Courses and the Intended Audiences

6. Is the course offered "direct to student" or through an existing college or university?

7. What is the primary intended student population—working adults in the United States (who more often than not study part-time), more traditional students (often but not always campus-based), or anyone and everyone with aptitude and interest all over the world?

8. To what extent can the course be adapted, or re-purposed, to serve other sets of students in the future, in various settings? There are important distinctions among online courses that are "home-grown," designed on an institution-specific platform that has little customization capacity, and

intended specifically for use by a known institutional population; online courses that are developed for a broader (and unknown) population of students; and online courses that are developed alongside, or on top of, a general platform but that have customizable features and allow for "local" varieties targeted at particular populations.

### Credentialing and Ownership

9. Does the course offer credit and a path to a degree, a certificate of accomplishment, or no credit or assessment of accomplishment?
10. Who owns (and/or has license to use) the intellectual property of the course materials? Is the controlling entity a for-profit or nonprofit organization?
11. What is the business model underlying the course offering? Is the course available to students for free, and if it is, who pays for the development and ongoing operation of the course?

There are obviously hundreds of possible permutations and combinations involving these and other distinctions. With so many dimensions along which online courses can be classified, a simple taxonomy can be both elusive and more confusing than helpful. The variety of online offerings is often underappreciated, as is the importance of deciding what characteristics are appropriate in a particular setting.

### Notes

1. William G. Bowen, *At a Slight Angle to the Universe: The University in a Digitized, Commercialized Age*, Romanes Lecture for 2000, University of Oxford, October 17, 2000 (Princeton, NJ: Princeton University Press, 2001), 24 (also available online at www.mellon.org/internet/news_publications/publications/romanes.pdf); "Teaching at an Internet Distance," University of Illinois faculty seminar, December 7, 1999, www.vpaa.uillinois.edu/tid/report.

2. Cited in Bowen, *At a Slight Angle to the Universe,* 23–24; Peter Navarro, "Economics in the Cyberclassroom," *Journal of Economic Perspectives* 14, no. 2 (Spring 2000): 129.

3. See Bowen, *At a Slight Angle to the Universe,* 24.

4. In the words of the authors of one study comparing face-to-face instruction with three different varieties of distance learning: "Like Campbell's Soups, distance learning now comes in so many varieties that it is increasingly difficult to generalize about it." (James V. Koch and Alice McAdory, "Still No Significant Difference? The Impact of Distance Learning on Student Success in Undergraduate Managerial Economics," *Journal of Economics and Finance Education* 11, no. 1 (Summer 2012): 36.)

5. This imagery is from Keynes's explanation of his difficulty rendering a portrait of Lloyd George at the Peace of Paris. John Maynard Keynes, *Essays in Biography* (New York: Horizon Press, 1951), 33. I shall offer one other snippet from this remarkable essay when I discuss collective decision-making.

6. "Changing the Economics of Education," interview with John Hennessy and Salman Khan, *Wall Street Journal,* June 4, 2012. See also Ken Auletta, "Get Rich U," *New Yorker,* April 30, 2012; Billy Gallagher, "Q&A: President John Hennessy on Online Education," *Stanford Daily,* October 30, 2012.

7. For a fuller study of barriers to adoption of online pedagogies, see Lawrence S. Bacow, William G. Bowen, Kevin M. Guthrie, Kelly A. Lack, and Matthew P. Long, *Barriers to Adoption of Online Learning Systems in U.S. Higher Education,* May 1, 2012, available on the ITHAKA website at www.sr.ithaka.org. The discussion in this book draws heavily on this report but is more cryptic and organizes the issues differently.

8. Kelly A. Lack, "Current Status of Research on Online Learning in Postsecondary Education." This is a revised version of a paper originally dated May 18, 2012, available at www.sr.ithaka.org/research-publications/current-status-research-online-learning-postsecondary-education.

9. In the widely cited SRI/DOE meta-analysis (usually cited as Means et al., 2009), most of the forty-six studies reviewed involved online learning in the fields of medicine or health care, and a great many studies compared the use of the two different modes of learning for less than a full semester. In addition, only twenty-five of the fifty-one online versus face-to-face comparisons analyzed in the meta-analysis involved undergraduate students. (The other twenty-six involved students in grades K–12, graduate students, or other types of learners.) See Barbara Means et al., *Evaluation of Evidence-Based Practices in Online Learning: A Meta-analysis and Review of Online Learning Studies* (Washington, DC: U.S. Department of Education, 2009), www2.ed.gov/rschstat/eval/tech/evidence-based-practices/finalreport.pdf.

10. In general, MOOCs are free or low-cost online courses that are available to interested users—in some cases, by the thousands, tens of thousands, or hundreds of thousands—throughout the world. These courses

typically consist of video lectures by well-known professors or experts in a particular field, often affiliated with elite institutions; the video lectures generally are complemented by problem sets and/or other assignments, and, in some cases, discussion boards where students can interact with one another asynchronously. Students typically have very little opportunity to interact with professors (with the exception, in some cases, of mass e-mails sent by the instructor to all enrolled students), though some instructors have teaching assistants available to answer questions or monitor the discussion boards. Completion of a MOOC is sometimes recognized with a certificate of accomplishment from the professor or from the MOOC itself, though it generally is not attached to credit from the college or university with which the professor is affiliated. See Lack, "Current Status of Research on Online Learning," for a description of varieties of online learning, including some of the best-known MOOCs. For an excellent summary of this terrain, see Laura Pappano, "The Year of the MOOC," *New York Times,* November 4, 2012. For a slightly earlier overview of the characteristics of, and the recent developments among, some MOOCs, see Abby Clobridge, "MOOCs and the Changing Face of Higher Education," *Information Today,* August 30, 2012, http://newsbreaks.infotoday.com/NewsBreaks/MOOCs-and-the-Changing-Face-of-Higher-Education-84681.asp. This field is changing so rapidly that there is one or another new development almost every day.

11. Khan Academy is undergoing an assessment, conducted by SRI International's Center for Technology in Learning, regarding the adoption and effectiveness of its materials in classrooms at twenty-one primary and secondary schools in Northern California during the 2011–12 year; a June 2012 newsletter said that a report was expected in December 2012, though as of early January 2013 no report had been published. (See "Research Update," SRI International, Center for Technology in Learning, June 2012, http://ctl.sri.com/news/newsletter_june_2012/june_2012_news.html.) With respect to the MOOCs offering college-level courses, both Coursera and edX have expressed an interest in working with ITHAKA on assessments, and a recent piece in the *Chronicle of Higher Education* reported that edX is planning to test a "flipped classroom" model—combining the use of content from its online courses with face-to-face teaching—at a community college. (Marc Parry, "5 Ways That edX Could Change Education," *Chronicle of Higher Education,* October 1, 2012.) According to an e-mail from Harvard's provost, Harvard has also developed "a course support model to assist faculty in thinking about what their own HarvardX courses might look like and to facilitate experimentation in course design" and is in the process of creating "a micro development environment" that will enable faculty to design courses and smaller pieces of courses called modules (Provost Alan M. Garber, e-mail to colleagues, November 16, 2012). (HarvardX is the Harvard organization responsible for the university's edX contributions and activities.) For-profit publishers active in this field have assembled some results that they claim, not surprisingly, make a case for their products. Disinterested third-party

assessments are clearly in order. See the appendix material in Lack, "Current Status of Research on Online Learning."

12. William J. Baumol, personal communication, November 7, 2012.

13. ITHAKA is a nonprofit organization created initially by the Andrew W. Mellon, William and Flora Hewlett, and Stavros Niarchos foundations. It is the parent of JSTOR and Portico and also operates an increasingly important strategy and research division (Ithaka S+R). Kevin M. Guthrie is the president of ITHAKA, and its board is chaired by Henry S. Bienen, president emeritus of Northwestern University. ITHAKA's mission is "to help the academic community use digital technologies to preserve the scholarly record and to advance research and teaching in sustainable ways."

14. The director and vice provost of the Carnegie Mellon's Open Learning Initiative (OLI) courses define a "cognitive tutor" as "a computerized learning environment whose design is based on cognitive principles and whose interaction with students is based on that of a human tutor, that is, making comments when the student errs, answering questions about what to do next, and maintaining a low profile when the student is performing well." They further explain that, unlike "traditional computer aided instruction," which "gives didactic feedback to students on their final answers," cognitive tutors "provide context-specific assistance during the problem-solving process." (Candace Thille and Joel Smith, "Learning Unbound: Disrupting the Baumol/Bowen Effect in Higher Education," Futures Forum, American Council on Education 2010, oli.cmu.edu/wp-oli/wp-content/uploads/2012/05/Thille_2010_Learning_Unbound.pdf, 34).

The director and vice provost also outline the process by which "feedback loops" can be used to support classroom learning: an instructor first assigns students to work through part of the OLI course, during which time the OLI system gathers, analyzes, and organizes data about the students' activities; the OLI system then presents the instructor with information about her students' learning for the instructor to review; and the instructor adapts her teaching as needed (ibid., 36).

15. See William G. Bowen, Matthew M. Chingos, Kelly A. Lack, and Thomas I. Nygren, "Interactive Learning Online at Public Universities: Evidence from Randomized Trials," May 22, 2012, available on the ITHAKA website at www.sr.ithaka.org. We are pleased to report that the study has been very well received by media outlets such as the *National Review,* the *Boston Globe,* the *Chronicle of Higher Education, Inside Higher Ed,* and, in particular, the *Wall Street Journal* (whose writer David Wessel called the report "carefully crafted" and its findings "statistically sound"). In addition to the six four-year institutions included in the study, we tried to include three community colleges. But for a variety of reasons—many logistical—this effort did not succeed, and we caution readers against simply extrapolating our findings to two-year colleges.

Courses like the CMU statistics course tested in this study exemplify what we call the interactive learning online (ILO) approach. This approach contrasts with more common types of online learning which often mimic classroom teaching without taking advantage of the unique online environment to provide "added value."

16. As can be seen from the figure, hybrid-format students did perform slightly better than traditional-format students on three outcomes—achieving pass rates that were about three percentage points higher, scores on the Comprehensive Assessment of Outcomes in Statistics (CAOS) that are about one percentage point higher, and final exam scores that are two percentage points higher—but none of these differences passes the usual tests of statistical significance. (The CAOS test is a standardized, 40-item multiple-choice assessment designed to measure students' statistical literacy and reasoning skills. In our study, we administered the CAOS test once at the beginning of the semester and again at the end of the semester. One characteristic of the CAOS test is that, for a variety of reasons, scores do not increase by a large amount over the course of the semester; among all the students in our study who took the CAOS test at both the beginning and the end of the semester, the average score increase was five percentage points. For more information about the CAOS test, see http://app.gen.umn.edu/artist/caos.html and Robert delMas, Joan Garfield, Ann Ooms, and Beth Chance, "Assessing Students' Conceptual Understanding after a First Course in Statistics," *Statistics Education Research Journal* 6, no. 2 (2007): 28–58.)

17. Thus, our finding is strikingly different in this consequential respect from an alternative (hypothetical) finding of "no significant difference" resulting from a coefficient of some magnitude accompanied by a very large standard error. A finding with big standard errors would mean, in effect, that we just don't know much—the "true" results could be almost anywhere.

18. We wondered if the opposite proposition would hold—that is, we thought it possible that students who are subject to what Claude Steele has called stereotype threat might actually do better in more anonymous settings. Not proven, is the verdict of this study. The size of our study, with over six hundred participants—roughly half in the "treatment" sections and half in the "control" sections—allowed us to look more carefully than most other studies have been able to do at these more refined groupings of students. We calculated results separately for subgroups of students defined in terms of characteristics including race/ethnicity, gender, parental education, primary language spoken, pretest score (that is, score on the first administration of the CAOS test), hours worked for pay, and college GPA. We did not find any consistent evidence that the hybrid-format effect varied by any of these characteristics (see Bowen et al., "Interactive Learning Online at Public Universities," table A6).

19. We also found, however, that students had a mild preference for traditional face-to-face instruction and that those in the hybrid-format sections thought that they had learned less, even though objective outcomes were essentially the same for students in the two groups. (See Bowen et al.,

"Interactive Learning Online at Public Universities," figure 3 and table A7.) A leader of one of the universities that participated in our study opined that a defect of the CMU prototype course is that it has no "addictive" or "Disney-like" appeal; it was, as this person put it, "designed by cognitive scientists" (no offense intended!). In contrast, some students in the traditional format may have been treated to an occasional colorful story, personal recollections of the instructor, or other practices that are sometimes used by faculty to make class more enjoyable and that have the effect of improving students' opinions of their course. The question of what is really going on here—with no differences in learning outcomes, as measured conventionally, combined with a (to be sure, small) difference in qualitative assessments—relates to a larger literature on objective measures of learning outcomes versus more subjective measures of student satisfaction (citations given in Bowen et al., "Interactive Learning Online at Public Universities," and in Lack, "Current Status of Research on Online Learning in Postsecondary Education").

20. The Khan Academy is a nonprofit that offers a free online library of more than three thousand short video lectures on a variety of topics. For some subjects, particularly those related to mathematics, Khan also provides practice exercises and data tools for instructors. For more information about the Khan Academy, see the appendix to part 2 of this book and the extended discussion of Khan's work in Michael Noer, "Reeducating Education," *Forbes,* November 19, 2012. In addition to the Khan Academy, Coursera, edX, Udacity, and other MOOC providers are working hard to garner evidence about what teaching methods work best. The potential for progress is considerable.

21. The existence of these and other problems probably explains, but only in part, the surprising lack of attention to costs among those who have studied online learning. Unfortunately, proponents of online learning often seem uninterested in costs. Carol Twigg at the National Center for Academic Transformation (NCAT) is an exception to this statement, and she deserves great credit for having focused on costs earlier than most people. However, the NCAT cost studies have been almost entirely self-directed by the institutions involved, which is far from ideal. Also, it is unclear in many cases whether initial successes with these courses were sustained. (See the discussion of the limitations of the NCAT studies in Lack, "Current Status of Research on Online Learning.")

22. The appendix material in Bowen et al., "Interactive Learning Online at Public Universities," presents these results and many more calculations, along with some graphs showing how sensitive potential savings are as we vary assumptions about section sizes and compensation.

23. Our results indicate that hybrid-format students took about one-quarter less time to achieve essentially the same learning outcomes as traditional-format students (Bowen et al., "Interactive Learning Online at Public Universities," 23).

24. Potential cost savings for both students and institutions are illustrated in an article on developments at the College of St. Scholastica, a parochial private college in Minnesota. See Paul Fain, "Another Push on Prior Learning," *Inside Higher Ed,* November 19, 2012. This college is a member of the Council of Independent Colleges, and Richard Ekman, the Council's president, has reported that several other member institutions are thinking along similar lines. This is a useful reminder that the private sector of higher education, including the small-college sector, has a big stake in these developments.

25. See John Laucrman, "Gates Backs MIT Online Course Offering at Community Colleges," *Bloomberg,* November 18, 2012, www.bloomberg .com/news/2012-11-18/gates-backs-mit-online-course-offering-at-community-colleges.html.

26. For an instructive account of the history of this course, which enjoyed large-scale support from the William and Flora Hewlett Foundation, see Taylor Walsh, *Unlocking the Gates* (Princeton, NJ: Princeton University Press, 2011), chapter 4.

27. See "Informing Innovation in Higher Education: Evidence from Implementing the Latest Online Learning Technologies in a Public University System," Ithaka S+R, November 13, 2012, www.sr.ithaka.org/news/ informing-innovation-higher-education-evidence-implementing-latest-online-learning-technologies.

28. Bowen et al., "Interactive Learning Online at Public Universities," contains a detailed discussion of the many lessons we learned along the way—including the importance of running pilots on each campus before conducting the research phase of the study. Others embarking on similar projects may find it valuable to ponder our missteps, most of which, fortunately, we were able to correct, following the pilots. We have great respect for other investigators who have coped with such problems, often in settings outside higher education.

29. Some careful work of this kind has been done. For example, an analysis by Shadish, Clark, and Steiner showed that, in some cases, the results of non-experimental studies can approximate those of experimental studies, particularly when a rich array of well-measured and well-chosen covariates is available, and when ordinary linear regression and/or propensity scoring are used to reduce bias. (See William R. Shadish, M. H. Clark, and Peter M. Steiner, "Can Nonrandomized Experiments Yield Accurate Answers? A Randomized Experiment Comparing Random to Nonrandom Assignment," *Journal of the American Statistical Association* 103 [2008] : 1334–56.) Similarly, when Shadish, Cook, and Wong (2008) examined twelve within-study comparisons of randomized and nonrandomized studies, they found that eight of these comparisons produced "reasonably close" results—with two of the remaining four comparisons having close results with respect to some analyses but not others, and the final two comparisons involving "particularly weak observational stud[ies]." (Thomas D. Cook,

William R. Shadish, and Vivian C. Wong, "Three Conditions under Which Experiments and Observational Studies Produce Comparable Causal Estimates: New Findings from Within-Study Comparisons," *Journal of Policy Analysis and Management* 27, no. 4 [2008]: 724–50.) More specifically, Shadish and his colleagues found that the three studies involving a regression-discontinuity design "produced essentially the same statistical significance patterns" as long as their analyses used the same assumptions as the experimental designs; that they "[could] also trust" the results from observational studies that minimized initial differences by matching intact control and treatment groups using some sort of baseline measure; and that even in cases where it was not possible to match treatment and control groups, identifying and measuring the correct selection process through the use of ordinary least squares regression, instrumental variables, or propensity score analyses allowed for the reduction of selection bias to some extent. The researchers concluded, "Taken as a whole, then, the strong but still imperfect correspondence in causal findings reported here contradicts the monolithic pessimism emerging from past reviews of the within-study comparison literature."

30. I am certainly not suggesting, however, that we abandon the search for rigor. I am suggesting that careful consideration be given to finding simpler approaches (as suggested in the previous note) that approximate the randomized trials model—perhaps by the use of well-chosen matching methods or lotteries in situations in which face-to-face courses are oversubscribed. There is also much to be said for quasi-experimental studies that use cut-offs and regression-discontinuity approaches. As my colleague Kevin M. Guthrie keeps pointing out, any kind of side-by-side test of different teaching methods is beset by complications. Ironically, it is much less problematic (though less instructive) just to substitute an entirely new approach for what was there before. Manifold issues that concern institutional review boards are thereby avoided. This is a bizarre state of affairs that deserves examination.

31. I refer here to the same *NEJM* article cited in part 1: Spencer S. Jones, Paul S. Heaton, Robert S. Rudin, and Eric C. Schneider, "Unraveling the IT Productivity Paradox—Lessons for Health Care," *New England Journal of Medicine* 366 (June 14, 2012): 2243–45.

32. See Daphne Koller and Andrew Ng, "Taking the Next Step in Online Education with Credit Equivalency," *Forbes*, November 16, 2012. At the same time, the time costs associated with taking MOOCs, which often require ten or more hours of work per week, are not negligible, and there are many students, particularly those who have part- or full-time jobs, who may simply not have the time to spend exploring new subjects through MOOCs, especially if they cannot earn credit for MOOC completion.

33. See Tamar Lewin, "College Credit Eyed for Online Courses," *New York Times*, November 13, 2012, as well as the official announcement of this project by Coursera and the discussion of this collaboration in Koller

and Ng, "Taking the Next Step." It is encouraging that a number of MOOCs are moving to address worries about cheating by requiring students to submit pictures of themselves with a form of photo identification via webcam, by sampling and comparing students' keystroke patterns, by arranging for either remote proctoring services or on-site proctoring of exams, or by other means. This development will surely increase the odds that some educational institutions will give credit, or at least advanced standing, to students who earn "certificates" of accomplishment or "badges" of some kind. (See Tamar Lewin, "Colorado State to Offer Credits for Online Class," *New York Times,* September 7, 2012; Steve Kolowich, "Site-Based Testing Deals Strengthen Case for Granting Credit to MOOC Students," *Inside Higher Ed,* September 7, 2012; Ki Mae Heussner, "5 Ways Online Education Can Keep Its Students Honest," *GigaOM,* November 17, 2012, http://gigaom. com/2012/11/17/5-ways-online-education-can-keep-its-students-honest/; and Nick Anderson, "Online College Courses to Grant Credentials, for a Fee," *Washington Post,* January 9, 2013.)

Kevin Carey of the New America Foundation has also cited the strong possibility that, over time, MOOCs will gain more and more acceptance, which he believes will lead to some "disintermediation" of educational services (separating credentialing from teaching) and, in turn, some cost savings for students and perhaps institutions. (Kevin Carey, "Into the Future with MOOCs," *Chronicle of Higher Education,* September 3, 2012.)

34. See Bacow et al., *Barriers to Adoption,* 21.

35. For a fascinating account of how one obviously talented professor of computer science at Vanderbilt University navigated this terrain, see Douglas H. Fisher, "Warming up to MOOCs," *Chronicle of Higher Education,* Professor Hacker blog, November 6, 2012. After describing his own initial reluctance to use the content of MOOCs created by others in his own courses (using much the same language that we used in our *Barriers to Adoption* report), Fisher decided that this attitude was just "silly," and he goes on to describe in great detail how he used Stanford course content highly effectively to "flip" his own classes. But Fisher also created his own "wrappers" for the material and obviously customized the content. He writes eloquently about how exciting he has found embracing the online content of others after years of being "alone in the wilderness." He now feels, he reports, as if he is part of a rich scholarly community whose members build on one another's best work. This is a highly praiseworthy attitude, I would submit, but it also reflects the considerable accomplishments and self-confidence of Professor Fisher—qualities not likely to be shared by anything like all professors at other colleges and universities.

36. Stanford president John Hennessy has lauded the social networking aspects of MOOCs as a source of added value, relative to what may be gained from more solitary online courses (as well as some face-to-face courses), specifically calling the speed with which MOOC students responded to each others' discussion board posts "phenomenal." (See

Salman Khan and John Hennessy, "Changing the Economics of Education," *Wall Street Journal,* June 4, 2012.)

Princeton professor Mitchell Duneier has described his experience teaching a Coursera course in similarly enthusiastic terms. (Mitchell Duneier, "Teaching to the World from Central New Jersey," *Chronicle of Higher Education,* September 3, 2012; see also quotations from Duneier in Tamar Lewin, "College of the Future Could Be Come One, Come All," *New York Times,* November 19, 2012.) In the *New York Times* article, Duneier is quoted as saying that within three weeks of starting to teach his course in introductory sociology, "I had more feedback on my sociological ideas than I'd had in my whole teaching career. I found that there's no topic so sensitive that it can't be discussed, civilly, in an international community."

EdX's Anant Agarwal also offers a helpful account of the value of peer-to-peer responses to questions in an online setting, describing the "fascinating" speed with which MOOC students answer each others' questions—even at 2 A.M. (See Tamar Lewin, "One Course, 150,000 Students: Q&A with Anant Agarwal," *New York Times,* July 18, 2012.) An irony not to be missed is that from this point of view, the more students, the better—in contrast to the usual desire to reduce class size in traditional teaching.

37. In his contribution to a Windsor Group study in 2007, President Hennessy both stressed the appeal of the idea of collaboration and explained why it is so hard to achieve when institutions have different needs and wish to exploit distinctive differences. (John Hennessy, "Technology and Collaboration: Creating and Supporting Public Goods," draft memos from Windsor Working Groups, September 24, 2007.)

38. Keynes, *Essays in Biography,* 39. I have often thought that private, family-run foundations yield other examples of the perils of collective decision-making absent a clear sense of direction and some precise location of authority.

39. Personal communication from the very able leader of the CMU project, Candace Thille, to Ira Fuchs, a member of the ITHAKA board, September 25, 2012.

40. For instance, one of the models proposed for Coursera involves providing a version of its platform and course content to community colleges to use in for-credit, low-cost courses for their own students; another proposed model would involve students at a particular university taking proctored exams upon completion of Coursera courses, in order to verify their skills in a certain area (so that, for instance, these students could receive a course waiver).

Likewise, at the time it was founded as a joint initiative of MIT and Harvard, edX's website said that edX would "begin by hosting MITx and Harvardx content, with the goal of adding content from other universities interested in joining the platform." (The precursor of edX, MITx, featured only MIT course content and was launched about half a year before the announcement of edX. The names MITx and HarvardX are currently used to refer to the course content from MIT and Harvard, respectively, that is hosted on the edX platform.) Since the announcement of edX in May 2012, edX has expanded to include several additional institutions. (See the appendix for more information about edX and its partner institutions.) Among edX's listed goals are to "expand access to education, allow for certificates of mastery to be earned by able learners, and make the open-source platform available to other institutions."

Finally, the website of Class2Go, Stanford Online's new internal platform, says that its creators "believe strongly that valuable course content shouldn't be tied to any one platform" and that Class2Go is open source in order to encourage others to use it, or "to work together with similar efforts in other places." (See Jeffrey R. Young, "Inside the Coursera Contract, How an Upstart Company Might Profit from Free Courses," *Chronicle of Higher Education,* July 19, 2012; "Online Course Hosting and Servicing Agreement," quoted in "The U. of Michigan's Contract with Coursera," *Chronicle of Higher Education,* July 19, 2012; "What is edX? Answering Common Questions about MIT and Harvard's New Partnership in Online Education," *MIT News,* May 2, 2012; and "Class2Go: Take Stanford Online Classes, Anywhere," Stanford University, 2012, http://class2go.stanford.edu.)

41. I do not regard the question of whether such an entity is for-profit or nonprofit as anything close to dispositive in thinking about possibilities for meeting the need I have just described. Indeed, I think that both structures have advantages as well as disadvantages. Once again, there is probably much to be said for healthy competition.

42. This is a real issue, which not even the prestige of MIT, Harvard, or Stanford can overcome readily. Senior academic leaders repeatedly expressed doubts about the wisdom of offering fully prepackaged courses to their students, citing a desire to "brand" courses as their own in order to preserve institutional identity. Of course, this problem would be alleviated greatly if established institutions were to grant credit to students who had earned certificates of accomplishment from MOOCs. But this is a challenging prospect in the case of most four-year institutions, at least without further testing by the institutions themselves or some other third-party method of certifying both the content of the course and the achievements of students taking the course. The collaboration between the ACE and Coursera (mentioned earlier) is encouraging in suggesting a path toward assessing both the credit-worthiness of online offerings and the success of students in passing these courses. Two-year institutions may be more likely than four-year institutions to move in this direction.

43. See Steven Kolowich, "How 'Open' Are MOOCs?" *Inside Higher Ed,* November 8, 2012, for a discussion of the extent to which outsiders are allowed to use MOOC content under various MOOCs' terms of service.

44. For a discussion of Coursera's thinking with respect to potential business models, including candid comments by Coursera's co-founders (Daphne Koller and Andrew Ng), see Young, "Inside the Coursera Con-

tract." While Coursera's courses are currently free to students, this may not always be the case; should Coursera start to charge for its courses, colleges that enter into contracts with Coursera might receive a portion of the revenues from those fees. (See Daphne Koller and Andrew Ng, "Log On and Learn: The Promise of Access in Online Education," *Forbes,* September 19, 2012.)

With respect to other prominent MOOCs, the leaders of edX have said that, in the near future, they will offer certificates to those who complete its courses for a "modest fee"; the extent to which students will be willing to pay for this certificate, however, remains to be seen. (See "Frequently Asked Questions," edX, www.edx.org/faq.) In addition, see Katherine Mangan, "Massive Excitement about Online Courses," *Chronicle of Higher Education,* October 1, 2012.

45. At his installation, MIT's new president, L. Rafael Reif, spoke explicitly about the need to address cost issues. (L. Rafael Reif, "Inaugural Address as Prepared for Delivery," Massachusetts Institute of Technology, Cambridge, MA, September 21, 2012, http://president.mit.edu/speeches -writing/inaugural-address.) As Stanford economics professor Caroline Hoxby has observed, it is surprising that many university leaders fail to analyze the cost and revenue implications of approaches to online learning before they invest in them (personal communication, September 21, 2012).

46. Thus, in the case of Khan Academy, it is hard not to wonder about the viability of Salman Khan's pronouncement: "Our mission statement is a free world-class education for anyone anywhere." (See "Changing the Economics of Education," interview by Walt Mossberg with John Hennessy and Salman Khan, *Wall Street Journal,* June 4, 2012.)

47. For example, among the learners who completed the circuits and electronics MOOC and who agreed to take a demographic survey, 96 percent said they had previously taken calculus, and about 70 percent had at least a bachelor's degree. This may not be surprising, given that the prerequisites for this course included (according to the course's website) an Advanced Placement–level physics course in electricity and magnetism, "basic" calculus and linear algebra, and "some background in differential equations."

A survey of students in Coursera's machine learning course revealed a somewhat different population, although this survey was not limited to learners who completed the course, and the main prerequisite for the machine learning course—a basic knowledge of programming—was, arguably, less restrictive than the prerequisites for the circuits and electronics course. The machine learning course survey revealed that among the more than 14,000 respondents, working professionals exceeded students, and among the students taking the course, the majority already had bachelor's degrees. (More specifically, 41 percent of all respondents said they were currently employed in the software industry, 9 percent said they were professionals employed in non-software areas of the computing and information technology industries, and 2.5 percent said they were employed in an industry other than technology. By contrast, about 20 percent of the respondents were graduate students, 11.6 percent were undergraduates, and 1 percent were enrolled in school at the K–12 level. See Steve Kolowich, "The MOOC Survivors," *Inside Higher Ed,* September 12, 2012; Steve Kolowich, "Who Takes MOOCs?" *Inside Higher Ed,* June 5, 2012.)

48. A recent *New York Times* article offers a useful overview of MOOC developers' search for ways to turn their courses' popularity into reliable sources of revenue. (Tamar Lewin, "Students Rush to Web Classes, but Profits May Be Much Later," *New York Times,* January 6, 2013.)

49. Someone asked, on Twitter, "Why would Antioch pay for something that is free?" The answer is that Coursera's terms of service prohibit (quite properly in my view) the use of Coursera's MOOCs for anything but informal education. These restrictions, which are characteristic of other MOOCs as well as Coursera, complicate the ability of colleges and universities to incorporate MOOC offerings in their regular for-credit curricula. (See Kolowich, "How 'Open' Are MOOCs?")

Readers interested in this subject should also see the op-ed piece in the *Wall Street Journal* on October 2, 2012 (in the online edition), by the new president of MIT, L. Rafael Reif, titled "What Campuses Can Learn from Online Teaching." Reif raises the possibility that "online education may improve the financial model of residential education." He envisions a world in which "a university's courses can be offered online for small fees to people around the world," and he suggests that "we might arrive at a sweet spot where high numbers of online learners are getting extremely good value for their fees, and the university that creates the content is using those fees to serve the mission of the university as a whole—part of which is to make education, on and off campus, affordable." In fact, Reif is not suggesting that everyone who registers for such a course be charged—which would contradict the notion that such courses are free—but that those who seek credentials certifying that they have mastered the content be charged a small fee for such certification. However, no one knows how such a plan would work in practice, and I continue to suspect that fees for institutional use of online courses may be a more viable way of addressing the various economic issues that confront us. Of course, it is conceivable that both individuals and institutions could be charged. Right now, all of this is highly speculative.

50. Bacow et al., *Barriers to Adoption,* 19–20.

51. Ibid., 29. One real problem is that ranking methodologies often focus on simple student-faculty ratios as measures of quality, and leaders at both private and public institutions understandably worry that online instruction may affect such ratios even if it does not affect learning outcomes. Equally deplorable is the exaggerated emphasis on SAT/ACT scores, which can lead to unwise admission decisions.

52. It is sobering to note the findings in a survey released in December 2012 by the Association of Governing Boards (AGB). While a majority of

the members of boards who responded said that higher education in general costs too much, an even higher percentage (62 percent) said that "their institution costs what it should." (Sara Hebel, "Board Members Say College Costs Too Much, but Not at Their Institution," *Chronicle of Higher Education,* December 13, 2012.) More awareness of the need to control costs "at home" is needed.

Another point worth reinforcing is the absence, from much of the discussion of the MOOCs' potential, of any emphasis on using such online offerings to save serious money on traditional campuses. The University of Texas System, which is now part of edX, is an exception to this generalization. The UT System is clearly interested in using MOOCs to "get more students through college more quickly and for less money." (See Steve Kolowich, "UT Hopes to Award Credit for Gateway edX Courses," *Inside Higher Ed,* October 16, 2012.) It remains to be seen, however, to what extent institutions in the UT System will, in fact, give credit for edX courses on an "as-is" basis, and to what extent (and at what cost) they will want to modify these courses to make course material developed largely for populations of students at Harvard and MIT useful to the much different student population in the UT System.

53. A majority (57 percent) of adults said they believed the U.S. higher education system was doing a fair or poor job of providing value for the money spent by students and their families, according to a spring 2011 survey by the Pew Research Center of more than two thousand adults. The proportion of adults agreeing that most people can afford to pay for college also fell from 39 percent in 1985 to 22 percent in 2011. (See Paul Taylor et al., "Is College Worth It?" Pew Research Center, May 15, 2011, www .pewsocialtrends.org/2011/05/15/is-college-worth-it/.)

54. An article in *Inside Higher Ed,* summarizing the results of a survey of faculty members on their attitudes toward the use of technology in education, defined "flipping the classroom" as "banishing the lecture and focusing precious class time on group projects and other forms of active learning." *Inside Higher Ed* was one of the two entities that conducted this survey; the other was the Babson Survey Research Group. (Steve Kolowich, "Digital Faculty: Professors and Technology, 2012," *Inside Higher Ed,* August 24, 2012.)

55. See Kolowich, "Digital Faculty"; I. Elaine Allen and Jeff Seaman, "Digital Faculty: Professors, Teaching, and Technology" (Babson Park, MA: Babson Survey Research Group and *Inside Higher Ed,* August 2012), http://babson.qualtrics.com/SE/?SID=SV_bJHd6VpmahG2NGB.

56. I discuss principles of delegation in chapter 2 of William G. Bowen, *Lessons Learned: Reflections of a University President* (Princeton, NJ: Princeton University Press, 2011). Of course, matters need not be, and should not be, so black and white; there is much to be said for nuance and the application of common sense. But I do understand why Gary C. Fethke and Andrew J. Policano (former interim president of the University of Iowa

and former dean of its business school, and current dean of the Paul Merage School of Business at the University of California, Irvine) bemoan an "hourglass" power structure, in which some kinds of authority are exercised solely by the regents at the top, and many other kinds of authority are exercised solely by the faculty, with the administration sometimes caught in the middle. (See Fethke and Policano, *Public No More: A New Path to Excellence for America's Public Universities* [Stanford, CA: Stanford University Press, 2012], 217.)

57. Let me give an example of sometimes troubling experiences JSTOR has had in attempting to explain the economic value of access to its digitized collections of scholarly literature. Sometimes (not infrequently) decisions as to whether to subscribe to a JSTOR collection are vested in the library and are thought about solely in terms of comparisons with the value of traditional acquisitions. This is much too limited an approach in that it does not take account of longer-term space savings (which are, one librarian told us, "no concern of his," since they come out of someone else's budget) or more complicated notions of the changing role of the library.

58. The course reinvention initiatives sponsored by the National Center for Academic Transformation (NCAT) generally focused on departments and thus led to situations in which the departments concerned captured all the savings. (See Ben Miller, "The Course of Innovation: Using Technology to Transform Higher Education," *Education Sector,* May 2010, www.icuf .org/newdevelopment/wp-content/uploads/2010/06/Technology-in-Higher -Ed.pdf, for a summary of several NCAT transformations.) It is easy to understand why this approach makes sense in terms of the desire to enlist support from faculty. But it does not address the more fundamental issue of saving costs for the institution at large or for students and families. Derek Bok has observed that "it will take rather adroit and firm leadership to capture the savings for institutions rather than have them disappear down the black hole of somewhat lower demands on the time of professors who teach these courses" (personal communication, October 30, 2012).

59. See American Association of University Professors, *1940 Statement of Principles on Academic Freedom and Tenure with 1970 Interpretive Comments* (January 1990), available at www.aaup.org/aaup/pubsres/ policydocs/contents/1940statement.htm; American Association of University Professors, *The Rights and Responsibilities of Universities and Their Faculties* (March 24, 1953).

60. Indeed, mistakenly equating academic freedom with unbridled faculty discretion, including control over methods of delivering classroom instruction, is dangerous and even self-defeating. The use of overly sweeping academic-freedom arguments to block reasonable efforts to innovate puts the core principles of academic freedom at risk.

61. A recent article in the *Economist* predicts that the unbundling prompted by the emergence and proliferation of MOOCs and other forms of educational technology will be coupled with increased specialization,

with some institutions "perhaps dropping indifferent lecturing or teaching to concentrate on something else, such as brilliantly set and marked examinations." Another likely result of unbundling is collaboration across institutions that recognize the value of pooling resources for purposes like offering common introductory-level undergraduate courses. ("Learning New Lessons," *Economist*, December 22, 2012.)

62. Joseph E. Aoun, "A Shakeup of Higher Education," *Boston Globe*, November 17, 2012.

63. Clay Shirky, "Napster, Udacity, and the Academy," blog post, November 12, 2012, www.shirky.com/weblog/2012/11/napster-udacity-and -the-academy/.

64. Not all institutions share this perspective; some top-tier institutions do not see a compelling reason to change their current operations. For example, according to the *Economist,* Oxford and Cambridge remain "determinedly unruffled" by the emergence of MOOCs: "Oxford says that MOOCs 'will not prompt it to change anything,' adding that it 'does not see them as revolutionary in anything other than scale.' Cambridge even says it is 'nonsense' to see MOOCs as a rival; it is 'not in the business of online education.'" While MOOCs are still a relatively new development, and may not currently pose a formidable threat to Oxbridge, steadfast resistance to adaptation in light of new technology may prove to be shortsighted. ("Learning New Lessons.")

65. Kevin M. Guthrie, president of ITHAKA, has written a thought-provoking paper on this general subject: "You Can Run But You Can't Hide: Colleges and the Forces of the Internet" (delivered at the 2012 Lafayette Conference on the Future of Liberal Arts Colleges, Lafayette College, Easton, PA, and to be published in *Education for an Uncertain World: The Future of the Liberal Arts College in the Age of Technology, Globalism, and Economic Challenge,* eds. Rebecca Chopp, Susan Frost, and Daniel H. Weiss [Johns Hopkins University Press, forthcoming]).

66. For examples of the power of inspired teaching in intimate settings, see William G. Bowen, "More to Hope than to Fear: The Future of the Liberal Arts College," presentation at the Lafayette Conference on the Future of Liberal Arts Colleges, Easton, PA, April 10, 2012, to appear in Chopp, Frost, and Weiss, *Education for an Uncertain World.*

We should not, however, exaggerate the distinction between what it is possible to achieve through inspired person-to-person exchanges and the rich interactions that are now possible (though by no means guaranteed) through online teaching. Princeton sociology professor Mitchell Duneier quotes a comment from one student who took the Coursera course that Duneier taught earlier this year to 40,000 learners in 113 countries: "It has been an incredible experience for me, one that has not only taught me sociology, but the ways other cultures think, feel, and respond. I have many new 'friends' via this class." (Duneier, "Teaching to the World from Central New Jersey.") This language is not all that different from what one might expect to hear from a student in a traditional classroom setting—and, of course, the students in this online course represented a wider range of perspectives than one could find in even the most diverse in-person setting. But then we also have to recognize that not all of Duneier's online students may have had this kind of experience.

67. Indeed, Stanford's medical school, with assistance from the Khan Academy, is experimenting with posting video lectures online for some of its classes. Instead of the professor's conveying the course content via live lectures (which, according to professors' estimates, about 70 percent of students do not attend), students watch the video lectures online before coming to class, and the professor devotes the in-person meetings to more interactive activities—such as meetings with patients, debates among students, and group exercises—that require students to apply what they learned from the video lectures. The professor leading this initiative has expressed hope that these online materials can be shared someday with similar medical schools, which teach essentially the same first- and second-year courses, as well as with medical professionals, both in the United States and around the world. (See "Medical Education at Stanford Gets More Interactive by Going Online," Stanford University, September 28, 2012, http://news.stanford .edu/news/2012/september/medical-education-online-092812.html.)

68. Quoted in John Hennessy, "Prepared Remarks for Commencement 2012," Stanford University, Stanford, CA, June 17, 2012, news.stanford .edu/news/2012/june/hennessy-commencement-remarks-061712.html.

69. Upon completing a Coursera MOOC on health care and the Affordable Care Act, Ursinus College politics professor Jonathan Marks wrote, "I am optimistic that this kind of MOOC will not eat my job because it and I are not really in the same business." Furthermore, he argued, MOOC providers will never replace traditional undergraduate institutions, because the "strongest" examples of the latter have "faculty and staff who have deliberated about" how to address students' "need to discover and bring to completion their best mature selves," and who "marshal the resources of the college, inside and outside of the classrooms, to fulfill their missions." By contrast, a typical MOOC provider offers "classes and teachers united by nothing apart from its platform to students who are expected to know what they want and to pursue it with minimal guidance." (See Jonathan Marks, "Who's Afraid of the Big Bad Disruption?" *Inside Higher Ed,* November 18, 2012.)

Marks is right to stress the importance of institutions' finding ways to teach students less tangible skills such as good judgment. Also, one can agree that "the capacity to decide what to think or how to act in areas, like health policy, where no formula can generate the right answer" may not lend itself especially well to being taught in a MOOC format. However, agreeing with this proposition does not negate the ability of MOOCs to impart useful knowledge of many other kinds to students in credit-bearing capacities. It is a mistake to be imprisoned in either-or thinking. The relevant question isn't whether a Coursera course will end the career of political science professors like Marks, or whether it will be able to offer the same kind of guidance as a more intimate face-to-face setting, but rather how to build portfolios of offerings best suited to different student populations and different settings.

70. To this Hutchins added, "Hard intellectual work is doubtless the best foundation of character, for without the intellectual virtues, the moral sense rests on habit and precept alone." (Robert Maynard Hutchins, *No Friendly Voice* [Chicago: University of Chicago Press, 1968], 93.)

71. Jeff Bezos, "We Are What We Choose," baccalaureate address, Princeton University, May 30, 2010, www.princeton.edu/main/news/archive/S27/52/51O99/index.xml.

72. The rush to participate in the "MOOC movement" no matter what (lest one be left behind) is a bit frightening. As the former acting president of Purdue University, Tim Sands, said at a discussion about online learning: "There's talk that if you're not in the game, you're going to miss the wave." (Elena Sparger, "President Sands and Panel Discuss Online Courses at President's Forum," *Purdue Exponent,* October 2, 2012.) Also see the highly publicized debate surrounding the (temporary) ouster of the president of the University of Virginia, and the conversation about the future of MOOCs at a recent conference at Cornell University. (Andrew Rice, "Anatomy of a Campus Coup," *New York Times,* September 16, 2012, www.nytimes.com/2012/09/16/magazine/teresa-sullivan-uva-ouster.html?pagewanted=all&_r=0; Akane Otani, "Cornell Professors Debate Future of 'Massive' Online Classes at University," *Cornell Daily Sun,* September 28, 2012.)

To exaggerate the dangers, but perhaps only slightly, consider this comment by Lawrence S. Bacow, former president of Tufts, after he had listened to one of the many discussions of what some see as the impending transformation of American higher education: "If I went to my board at Tufts and told them that I was purchasing an enterprise software system on which the entire revenue stream depended, and that the vendor had been in business for less than a year and had no track record, revenue, or business model, I suspect I would have been fired. Yet some boards are forcing their presidents to contemplate hugely consequential changes in strategy based on six months' worth of experience from a handful of MOOCs." (Lawrence S. Bacow, personal communication, October 2, 2012.)

73. For an excellent example of the time it takes to do good work in this field, see the account of Neil Heffernan's work on tutoring models cited in Annie Murphy Paul, "The Machines Are Taking Over," *New York Times,* September 14, 2012. Heffernan has been working for seventeen years on what appears to be a highly promising way of using machine-guided tutoring to teach math. James Kemple, executive director of the Research Alliance for New York City Schools, also argues persuasively that "effective, sustainable reform requires persistence and adaptation, which must be informed by the accumulation of evidence, over time, about what seems to be working and what doesn't." (See James Kemple, "Math Innova-

tion Requires Patience," *New York Times,* SchoolBook blog, September 21, 2012, www.schoolbook.org/2012/09/19/innovation-in-math-instruction -deserves-patience-and-persistence.) Kemple is critical of two of the original School of One schools for deciding to discontinue the School of One program before they had an opportunity to incorporate ongoing improvement efforts and assess them. (School of One is a middle-school mathematics program used in some New York City public schools that emphasizes the use of technology to allow for more individualized learning.)

74. See Miller, "The Course of Innovation."

75. See I. Elaine Allen and Jeff Seaman, *Changing Course: Ten Years of Tracking Online Education in the United States* (Babson Park, MA: Babson Survey Research Group, 2013), 17. The authors of this report, which was put together by the Babson Survey Research Group in partnership with the Sloan Consortium and Pearson, differentiate between traditional, "web-facilitated," hybrid, and online courses on the basis of the proportion of content delivered face-to-face versus online (according to survey respondents); "online courses," by the authors' definition, are those in which at least 80 percent of the course content is delivered online.

76. The Open University's website is www.open.ac.uk. David L. Kirp chronicles the development of OU in chapter 10 of *Shakespeare, Einstein, and the Bottom Line: The History of Higher Education* (Cambridge, MA: Harvard University Press, 2003). See also "Europe Starts to Embrace Online Education," *Science 2.0,* September 28, 2012, www.science20.com/news_ articles/europe_starts_embrace_online_education-94485.

77. See Indiana University, "Indiana University Announces IU Online, A Major New Online Initiative," September 5, 2012. The pressures on universities to join the MOOC movement are illustrated well by a recent forum at Cornell University; see Otani, "Cornell Professors Debate Future of 'Massive' Online Classes at University."

78. See Thille and Smith, "Learning Unbound," 31–38, for a description of the features of the Open Learning Initiative courses. Also see chapter 4 of Walsh, *Unlocking the Gates,* for a description of the development of the Open Learning Initiative.

79. While the examples provided here generally involve prominent institutions, it is not only the big-name universities that have shown an interest in MOOCs. For example, the University of Maine at Presque Isle has announced an initiative that will "allow learners of all ages to participate in online college courses for free, as long as they aren't seeking college credit." Initially, the project will involve a slate of English courses, and care is being taken to avoid copyright issues. (See Jen Lynds, "UMPI OpenU expands access to college-level courses for free," *Bangor Daily News,* August 16, 2012, http://bangordailynews.com/2012/08/16/news/aroostook/ umpi-openu-expands-access-to-college-level-courses-for-free/.)

80. See Hannah Seligson, "10 Universities to Form Consortium for Online Courses," *New York Times,* November 15, 2012.

# Discussion by Howard Gardner

I AM HONORED to have been invited to comment on Bill Bowen's first Tanner Lecture. The lecture is witty, insightful, authoritative. I had the privilege of reading the lecture in draft form and I can assure you that it contains an entire education about the financing of universities. In fact there is an additional education in the endnotes alone, more than seventy-five of them.

During the 2012 presidential election, Big Bird was in the news. Whether or not you were a regular viewer of *Sesame Street,* you probably know the game featured there: "One of these things is not like the others, one of these things just doesn't belong." As I read through Bill's learned lecture, I kept hearing this musical refrain.

I heard this lingering melody because, unlike Bill Bowen and John Hennessy, I have not been a respected president of a major university. Truth to tell, except for my own small research group, I've never run anything! In fact, come to think of it, I've never even been *asked* to run anything—let alone a flagship university like Princeton or Stanford.

To add insult to injury, I am not in any sense an expert on the financing of universities, on cost and productivity. What I know is what I read in the *New York Times* and what I learned from Bill Bowen's text and footnotes. And so I am not going to take your time simply paraphrasing, if not bundling or bungling, his address.

Now that I have confessed to my disqualifications, let me attempt to atone.

My remarks today are bookended by conversations with two very bright and very self-confident recent young graduates.

Graduate #1 came to see me. I'll call him Jerry. Jerry announced that he had just completed an educational intervention that had "transformed" the secondary schools in a developing country. Now, he indicated, he wanted to transform collegiate education in America. "Dr. Gardner," said Jerry, "colleges and universities in America now cost over $50,000 a year. No one can or should lay out that huge sticker price. And so I am creating a system where high school graduates can get a first rate college education . . . for $5,000 a year."

I listened for a while and then said, "Jerry, there's one thing you haven't talked about yet. Is this college of the future going to be simply a gathering place for people who already live in an area like metropolitan Boston or San Francisco, or will it be residential for students from all over the country and the world?"

Jerry paused for a moment before he confessed, "Gee, I hadn't thought of that."

I want to speak today about residential education: the cons, the pros, its possibilities, single and collaborative, local and global.

Even when I went to college, Harvard College, over fifty years ago, we used to joke that we did not need faculty or courses. All we needed were our peers, who, needless to say, were as brilliant and talented as we deemed ourselves to be—our peers and Widener Library. One could repeat the wisecrack today, although, with all of the information available from search engines, we would not even need Widener—just guys, gals, and Google.

An interesting thought experiment: What would a post-secohdary school institution be if you just made it possible for students to be together for twenty-seven or thirty-six months over three or four years? Would it be closer to Plato's Academy or to William Golding's *Lord of the Flies*?

We do know that there are some less than palatable conse-quences of having students domiciled together. There is a lot of drinking, a lot of carousing, too much hazing and sexual harassment. Recently, as many of you may have heard, a huge cheating episode involving a take-home examination was uncovered at Harvard. I've done quite a bit of probing into the episode: there is little question that it was facilitated by the residential character of Harvard College. Apparently students shared notes, met with one another and with the teaching fel-lows, and had a well-greased network for disseminating infor-mation, if not the precise answers to the exam (including, as it turned out, inadvertently sharing typographical errors).

Of course, cheating can take place in nonresidential envi-ronments. Indeed, the proprietors of online learning networks are already taking steps to prevent or reduce the amount of cheating in MOOCs.

My purpose here is not to undermine residential educa-tion. But I need to point out that it is not a panacea. Jerry's goal (let's call it "the best of Williams") will not be instantly solved if he manages to fashion a less expensive form of residen-tial education—a kind of fast-food tertiary institution, named McWilliams or McYale or, if you'll excuse the wretched pun, McMacalaster.

Many of us who had the privilege of a four-year residential education appreciated our opportunities, even as those who did not have the privilege, or who feel that they wasted it, lament the loss. The challenge is to capture the best features of residential education while reducing or eliminating those that are not quintessential or not desirable, or, as Bill Bowen has insisted, are simply too costly.

And just what are those features? Here I could simply refer you to Andrew Delbanco's excellent recent book *College,* but let me present my own short list:

1. The opportunity to spend extended periods of time with scholars from different disciplines and perspectives: learning what they do and how they do it; having a chance to become part of the process of mastering established lore and of creating new knowledge.

2. The opportunity not only to master one subject area, one discipline, but also to sample areas of knowledge that broaden one's perspective, to synthesize that knowledge, and to participate in a culminating or capstone course, of the sort that was common a century ago.

3. The opportunity to live in close proximity to peers who come from very different backgrounds and have different life experiences and aspirations. Not just living, but sitting next to these peers in class and having the chance to exchange views and, at times, to disagree, in a respectful fashion.

4. The chance to receive intelligent, personalized feedback on work and on projects, with the opportunity for face-to-face, eyeball-to-eyeball discussions with teachers and peers.

5. The chance to participate in, and perhaps even initiate, activities that are fun, activities from which one can learn, and activities that serve the wider community.

6. Last but perhaps most valuable: the creation and maintenance of a community that embodies the best of human values—intellectual, social, and ethical. Recognizing that the outside world falls short, but that a better community is possible, is a crucial lesson that can be conveyed through

high-quality residential education. This is a reason why alumni so often return to campus; they think of their college experiences as the best years of their lives.

Sounds great—let me enroll. But even if we do not have in mind Tom Wolfe's dystopian novel *I Am Charlotte Simmons,* we need to make a confession. Most of our tertiary institutions, indeed most of our very best tertiary institutions, have fallen very, very far from these six ideals.

I don't know whether it was ever much better. In fact, truth to tell, I don't even *care* whether it was ever much better than it is now. What I do know is that the aforementioned sextet of ideals are often honored more in the breach than in the observance. A few of our institutions are likely to survive for a while, especially if they have ten- or twenty- or thirty-billion-dollar endowments. But the vast majority of tertiary institutions, which number in the many hundreds, are at great risk unless they come closer to these ideals. Unless they can actually prove to a skeptic that their residential education is worthwhile, indeed—truth to tell—if they, if we, are to retain our highly valued tax-free status.

What might be done to preserve the best of residential education and to make it less expensive? I will not try to legislate for other places, but let me tell you what I'd recommend for Harvard, the place that I know the best.

1. Hire and retain only those scholars who want to teach, who get a kick out of teaching, and who like spending time with students. As I phrase it in the Boston area, More local, less Logan.
2. Present subjects in ways that connect to the lives of students and to the options that they will face. Ninety-five percent of students are not going to be miniature versions of their professors, and it is not fair to treat them as if that is what they are aspiring to be.

3. At the same time, don't simply become vocational or pre-vocational. If McDonalds or McKinsey or Morgan Stanley wants to run their own colleges, let them.

4. Embrace distance learning, let it do what it can do, and save your time and effort for what cannot be achieved, with quality, online.

5. Create time and space for extracurricular activities, but don't allow them to dominate the students' time. Extra should mean *extra* in the sense of *added,* not merely *outside of.* Do not admit students primarily on the basis of their nonscholarly gifts, and don't allow them to segregate themselves on that basis. Personally, and here I know I am stepping on many toes, I would recommend having only intramural sports, in the spirit of Swarthmore and the University of Chicago.

6. Cut the frills. I can't do the cost analysis, but there is no reason why our elite schools need to be competing with the Marriott Hotel chains, let alone the Four Seasons. Or, if schools insist on keeping these frills—the top floor of the dormitory, so to speak—then charge those who want them multiples more for that privilege: $250 a day for Marriott College, $500 a day for Four Seasons University.

7. Cut the support staff while making sure that the primary mission has been preserved.

8. Develop and maintain a community that embodies the most admirable values of society; become shareholders in this community, create the norms together, and make sure that they are known, maintained, enforced, and, as appropriate, revised. Until recently, I did not devote attention to honor codes and codes of respect. I now believe that they are important, indeed essential—and places like Harvard, which don't have them, are delinquent. Wherever it may be housed, Jerry's college will need such a code as well.

On support staff, a short anecdote: A scholar friend of mine wanted to know how many support staff there were in the central headquarters of the New York City public schools. Turns out there were thousands. He decided to get a comparable number from the parochial schools. He kept going back to the same informant, who said that she did not have the figure. He persisted and persisted. Finally, she said "Okay," and closed her eyes. "Let me count them," she said. "I think there are twenty-seven."

You may well be thinking, well, Howard Gardner sure has a lot of advice, but on the basis of what? Here I draw on almost twenty years of research in the United States on what it takes to develop good workers, good citizens, and good persons. What can I say on the basis of this research?

Many students in elite schools are searching for admirable role models. If they take the time to get to know teachers, and vice versa, it turns out to be tremendously rewarding on both sides. The establishment of reflection sessions—students and faculty facilitators participating in discussions about important life choices somewhere in between classes and bull sessions— can be worthwhile, even transformative. We've done this for freshmen at Harvard, and last year Stanford adopted similar ones. It is worth trying to establish a commons—a real and a virtual space where members of a community can identify dilemmas and try to resolve them, drawing on the wisdom, rather than the tyranny, of crowds.

I'd like to mention one other line of research in which my colleagues and I have been involved. It entails collaboration among tertiary institutions. At wealthy schools like Harvard, Princeton, or Stanford, collaboration used to be an option: fine if you do it, fine if you don't. But even the most wealthy and the most vainglorious institutions now realize that they can no longer afford to go it alone. For 150 years, Harvard and MIT have been located within a few miles of one another, but only in the last few years has the vital importance of collaboration come to be appreciated. And so there are already impressive collaborations, like the Broad Institute in biomedical science, and promising collaborations, like edX, with its tributaries at MIT, Harvard, and a rapidly growing set of other tertiary institutions.

But I want to mention two other kinds of collaborations. Ten miles west of Cambridge are three schools whose collective geographical span is less than that of the campus of the University of Michigan in Ann Arbor. There are Wellesley College, a liberal arts school known to all of you; Babson College, a business school with an emphasis on entrepreneurship; and Olin College, a still new and innovative engineering school with a commitment to a broad, interdisciplinary education.

In the last few years, these schools have embarked on an ambitious collaboration to enrich the experiences of students. The BOW collaboration, as we've dubbed it, has the advantage that the schools are almost ideally complementary. That is, with their different foci, there is little overlap or competition. In this respect they differ from collaborations among similar liberal arts institutions, like Swarthmore, Haverford, and Bryn Mawr. And so students can really have experiences on one campus that they could not have on another. Moreover, certain issues of our time are ideally suited for such multicampus work. The first identified issue has been sustainability. I trust you can see how the input from business, engineering, economics, demography, and sociology is all relevant to the achievement of sustainability. Many other problem areas, of the sorts to which aspiring citizens naturally gravitate, can also benefit from the kind of multidisciplinary, multicampus collaboration fashioned in the BOW spirit.

America is a highly individualistic society, perhaps the most individualistic in the world. To paraphrase that noted educational philosopher, Finley Peter Donne, known more familiarly as Mr. Dooley, "Collaboration ain't beanball." To get the financial arrangements in order is not easy, even for the heating of buildings or the shoveling of snow (not a problem in Palo Alto, to be sure). To get calendars aligned risks giving heart attacks to faculty and to registrars. Joint hiring of faculty, granting of certificates or even degrees, and common grading rubrics require the diplomatic skills of Secretary of State James Baker, Senator George Mitchell, and United Nations chief Dag Hammarskjöld. (And ultimately it can save a lot of money, lowering that denominator which properly concerns Bill Bowen.) And yet the synergies across three different institutional cultures, each with its own residential flavor, can be considerable. The BOW experiment is worth watching and, if it goes well, worth emulating in any jurisdiction with more than a single tertiary institution.

Very much in passing, let me mention one last form of collaboration: that involving tertiary institutions in different countries, continents, and hemispheres. (We'll leave aside planets or galaxies for now, unless NYU President John Sexton happens to be listening or perhaps seated somewhere in this auditorium, or even floating above us!) The problems of collaboration that I have just mentioned are compounded when one wants to unite NYU and Abu Dhabi, Cornell and Qatar, Yale and Singapore, or MIT and Singapore—and, though I don't know it for a fact, Singapore is probably looking at Stanford and Princeton as well. International collaborations have the enormous dividend of exposing American students to dramatically different populations and cultural settings. And of course international students can add tremendous value to our sometimes highly parochial college campuses.

To be sure, there have always been study-abroad programs, and these have yielded dividends for those who take them seriously. But the opportunity to reach beyond Florence or

Barcelona, to have genuinely joint degrees, to share resources both over distances and face to face, to work together on problems that are global and require genuinely interdisciplinary and intercultural thinking, opens up vistas not imaginable fifty years ago. Perhaps they can even give a new meaning to the phrase *residential education,* or, if I can be permitted a neologism, *coresidential education.*

Well, I hope I've succeeded in hiding my ignorance of issues of costs and productivity in higher education. I've sought to do so by focusing on what, under the best of circumstances, can and should be achieved by residential education and perhaps doing so at significantly less cost, with perhaps, as a bonus, significantly more rewards—even more productivity!

Back at the start of my talk, I mentioned Jerry, the recent graduate who had great plans to undercut Stanford and Princeton but had not thought about where his imagined college might be domiciled. Let me close with the story of another encounter, with another bright and self-confident young man.

I had given a talk about the kinds of minds that we need to cultivate in the future. After the talk, this young man—we'll call him Larry—came up to me and said, "Professor Gardner, here's my smartphone. Why do we need to have school at all? After all, this device contains answers to all the questions one might ask."

I paused for a moment, looked Larry squarely in the eye, and then said, "Yes, the answers to all questions—except the important ones."

The series in which I'm privileged to be a commentator is called the Tanner Lectures on Human Values. In our economically oriented and productivity-obsessed environment, we need to pause to think about the meanings of the word *human* and of the word *values.* Distance learning has great potential; an accounting system has its place. But if our tertiary institutions are to retain their primary reasons for existing, we need to insist on the rights and responsibilities of human beings and on the place of values in our brief time on the planet. And if our esteemed educational institutions are to live up to their vaunted reputations, they must remain not only the repository but also the embodiment of what humans can aspire to.

# Discussion by John Hennessy

**LET ME PROPOSE,** as a beginning point, that we should all accept the premise that a residential liberal arts education is the gold standard to which higher education should aspire. The challenge we face in an increasingly economically challenging time is: how do we preserve as much of that gold standard as we possibly can? We understand, just like gold jewelry, there will be 24-karat, 18-karat, and 10-karat organizations, and then there will be those that simply have a little gold plate on the outside. I would like to ask what we can do to preserve the best possible program for the highest number of students.

Let us start with the question that Professor Bowen raised yesterday. Is there a cost problem in higher education? I think the answer to that is undeniably there is a cost problem but with many caveats around the structure of that cost problem. In a wonderful book, *Why Does College Cost So Much?*, two colleagues, Professors Robert B. Archibald and David H. Feldman, plotted lines of the growing cost of higher education and demonstrated that in fact, higher education had much the same cost structure as other service industries that relied on highly educated people. The good news was that we were no more expensive in terms of cost growth than dental services, and we were better than lawyers! However, we were worse than doctors in terms of cost growth, and I will come back to this as a way of thinking about what we could do about the cost challenges in higher education.

The core problem is that the sticker price of a college education is going up faster than the consumer price index (CPI) and even the wage inflation index; the difficulty is compounded by what has happened with family income and family dynamics. Professor Bowen pointed out yesterday the flattening of family income that has occurred over the last decade, but there is another issue that I think is not mentioned very often but played a significant role in the period from the 1960s through to the 1990s, and that was the reduction in family size, which meant that families actually had more money per child to spend on higher education. But family size has stopped shrinking more recently. Both factors have contributed to making affordability even more challenging.

Just how fast is the sticker price going up? Amazingly, despite the existence of antitrust agreements, many higher education institutions seem to raise their tuition at remarkably similar rates. The feedback effect is clearly operating here. If you look at those numbers over a thirty-year period, Stanford's tuition has gone up 2.8 percentage points per year above CPI, and over a total of thirty years, that is an astonishing differential growth rate. The relationship between sticker price, net price, and expenses is complex.

### The Role of Financial Aid and State Subsidies

Let's start with net tuition because it is an important metric. Net tuition takes the average tuition paid by a student (before financial aid) and subtracts the average financial aid. Only institutional or federal scholarships are counted as financial aid; loans are not. (Net tuition is a slightly misleading figure

**Figure 5** List price, financial aid, and net tuition at Stanford over thirty years, compiled from Stanford's university budgets

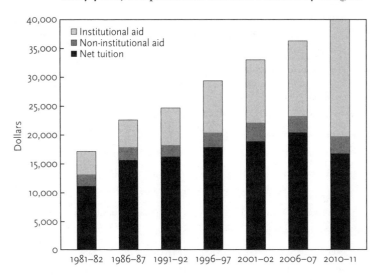

because recently, as the number of low-income students has gone up, and lower-income families have grappled with the cost of room and board, many institutions have begun subsidizing room and board. In a net tuition calculation, this subsidy appears to reduce tuition. For residential institutions, net total cost of attendance may be a better metric.)

If you look at Stanford's net tuition (figure 5), it has gone up in the most recent thirty-year period at a rate that is 1.4 percentage points above CPI, which means that financial aid increases have covered 50 percent of the list-price tuition growth. The most interesting period, however, is between 2006 and the present, when net tuition actually dropped to a level that roughly equals what it did in 1994 inflation-adjusted dollars. There actually was a decrease in net tuition enabled by a significant increase in institutional financial aid. That financial aid brought our net tuition number down to about $16,500, compared with a sticker price of just over $40,000.

This, of course, is a Stanford number. You can think about financial aid among the private institutions as a three-tier system, with Stanford and most of the Ivy League in the top tier. The next tier is a group of institutions which give significant amounts of financial aid but perhaps not as much, particularly at some of the upper income levels, that is, in the $100,000 to $150,000 range of family income. Then there is a group of universities and colleges that cannot possibly provide this level of financial aid; most of them are characterized by the fact that 75 percent or more of their revenue comes directly from tuition dollars. The only way they can significantly raise their financial aid package in that third tier is by subsidizing one student's financial aid using the sticker-price tuition payments of another student.

Now, total cost of attendance is not $40,000, which is only tuition, but closer to $52,000, including room and board and other associated expenses, and net cost of attendance is not $16,500 but $28,600. There is a significant difference between net tuition and net cost of attendance because many low-income students are getting significant amounts of financial aid toward their room and board and other costs. Nonetheless, net total cost of attendance (that is, the total cost of attendance after all financial aid sources are removed) is still lower than it was about a decade ago. Remember, this is the high end of the financial aid spectrum. You might ask how this significant increase in financial aid has been funded and whether or not such funding is sustainable. It has, as Professor Bowen observed yesterday, been funded by a significant growth in endowment. Endowment has grown on a per-student basis at roughly 6 percentage points over the higher education price index (HEPI), which tends to be 0.5 to 1 percentage point over the wage inflation index. Over a long period of time, HEPI has grown at a rate 1.5 percentage points above increases in the CPI. A key question is whether this record of strong endowment growth will continue. The rapid growth above inflation and payout has dramatically shifted the university budget over thirty years: in 1981–82, 6 percent of our budget came from endowment income. This past year (2011–12), 21 percent of our budget came from endowment income.

[*Audience question*] Does that include research expenses?

Yes, that includes research in the overall budget. Externally funded research fell from 42 percent to 33 percent over a comparable period, with endowment making up most of that difference, along with clinical income from the medical school. Untangling the finances when you have a medical school is difficult, but we can do it, at least approximately. Because universities archive lots of information, you can actually go back and get the budget of thirty years ago, and while not all the fund sources are identical, you can do a fairly good comparison over a long period.

It is the growth in endowment that has allowed the financial aid programs to increase significantly. Nonetheless, we, like many other institutions, are currently paying a significant fraction (roughly 25 percent) of our undergraduate financial aid budget out of temporary reserves, for the simple reason that we are in this recovery process from the 2008 financial crisis and recession, which drove down the value of the endowment. There is also a lingering effect in terms of family income and assets, which has increased our financial aid demands by about $10 million a year.

The public institutions are in a much more complicated situation. They have gone through a series of annual budget cuts, amounting to a significant fraction of their overall subsidy from the state. Overall, the average net tuition in inflation-adjusted dollars is roughly where it was in the mid-1980s, but the path over the last twenty-five years has not been smooth. In the 1980s, as state budgets grew, more and more money went into higher education. The net cost for attendance actually dropped from 1985 until the late 1990s, and then it began a steep uphill rise. Part of the public reaction that we see is to this steep increase that has occurred over the past ten to fifteen years. For better or worse, a series of zero or below-inflation increases in the 1980s and early 1990s significantly increased the dependence of the educational budget on the states. The problem occurs now, when increases of 20 to 25 percent are required to make up for decreases in state subsidy. Had tuition been raised at same rate as the wage inflation index, the problem and sense of crisis would be smaller.

The average grants and average loans for college students have grown about equally over time, so while there is a lot of angst over loans, the case is way overstated, in my view. Professor Bowen alluded to the *New York Times* article that was focused on finding the worst cases. Today, 73 percent of the students who attend nonprofits graduate with a debt balance of less than $25,000, and roughly 40 percent graduate with less than $10,000 of debt. There is a problem, which is at the for-profit institutions; I will return to this shortly.

The overall budget problem at public institutions is serious, and I am pessimistic about the possibilities for fixing it. On average, the public research universities have seen about a 15 percent real decrease in their per-pupil funding. There are lots of alternative numbers that get quoted. A percentage of the total budget that the state pays is frequently used, but it is not a good indicator of the state's investment in undergraduate education, because the research establishments have grown so large.

Why have states decreased the per-student funding by 15 percent? Let's put aside the 2008 financial crisis and its particular impact on state pensions, since much of that is yet to be accounted for. There is another insidious factor, and that is the rising Medicaid spending, and that has gone from roughly 0.2 percent to roughly 0.9 percent of the average state budget. This quadrupling in a period of thirty years has made other investments more difficult. This gets back to a point that Professor Bowen made yesterday: How do we, as a society, think about investing the tax revenues that we have? We have to make an important set of decisions, because entitlements will consume every dollar of tax revenue unless we tame their growth. Both the states and the federal government will be affected by these trends.

While I think we still have good affordability at the present time, we do have a growing problem: full sticker price is going up significantly faster than inflation, and the revenue sources that have allowed us to subsidize that list price (rapid growth of endowment in the case of the privates and state financing in the case of the publics) are both endangered. Thus, unless we do something significant, more students will be paying closer to sticker price, and that price will continue to escalate faster than family income.

## Cost Drivers of Sticker Price

So why is sticker price going up so fast? Professor Bowen touched on the key issues: wages, driven by the competition for an elite workforce. Faculty salaries have gone up faster than wages for most other workers in this country. Those of us who have been in the academy long enough realize that, financially, life is much more pleasant now than it was thirty years ago. Of course, the labor market for faculty largely drives this, and I think trying to swim upstream against the market, whether you are capping wages or you are capping the price of gasoline, does not work well.

Second, we have seen few or no productivity gains in higher education, at least as measured in traditional ways (e.g., dollars per student degree). Look at what has happened with other skilled workforces: doctors, dentists, and lawyers. They have all introduced assistant-level positions: physician assistants, paralegals, and dental hygienists, whose function is to offload the more expensive and more skilled worker, reducing the cost of a service. We sometimes pursue similar routes in the academy using adjunct professors and graduate students. Unfortunately, from a cost perspective, in most of our institutions, the offloading of faculty has been replaced not with other teaching requirements for that faculty member but with a growth in research as a fraction of the faculty member's time.

I am going to come back to the costs imposed by research, but first let me talk about other services we provide for students. I think the real driver of cost in other services is the need for additional services with a student body that is very different than it was thirty or forty years ago. Contrary to the writing of some pundits, the expenditure is not for luxury suites and climbing walls. We do not offer a "Four Seasons experience": our freshmen all share rooms with bathrooms down the hall, and I assure you that even though more than half of them had their own room and probably their own bathroom before they arrived here, they seem perfectly happy. But there are real costs, and I believe those costs come from the changing nature of the student body. We have a much larger fraction of low-income, first-generation students, and as Professor Bowen has argued, that is a good thing for the country, but he also mentions in his book *Crossing the Finish Line* that there are costs associated with these demographics.

Another issue, which I think all universities have experienced, is a rise in expenses related to student mental health. Students who previously never got to an elite college because they could not be competitive enough to get through high school at the top of their class can now get through high school with the help of various psychological support services, but they arrive at college facing many challenges. You could continue down the list. For example, community centers and ethnically themed dorms help acclimate and support students from diverse backgrounds. These services help create an environment which ensures that more students graduate and succeed, but they have additional costs associated with them.

There is another cost factor we can look at, and it is one that Professor Bowen alluded to: the cost of being a research institution. I have come to believe that as a country we are simply trying to support too many universities that are trying to be research institutions. The costs are truly significant, and incremental. Research is an activity that must be subsidized. I did a back-of-the-envelope calculation to try to look at the costs of having a research-oriented institution. I took Berkeley, a great institution, and my argument in no way should be taken to mean that we should stop having institutions like Berkeley; it is rather just an example of estimating what it costs to run a research institution. Down the road another twenty-five miles from here is San Jose State, an institution whose research budget from external sources is less than one-tenth of what Berkeley's is. San Jose State is primarily an educational institution, with no PhD programs, simply a set of master's programs and undergraduate programs. These are two institutions in the same region with a similar cost of living.

Let's look at both student-faculty ratios and costs per student as metrics. I decided an adjustment was appropriate for PhD students, so I counted each PhD student at Berkeley as the equivalent of two undergraduates or master's students. After making these adjustments, let's consider the university budget per FTE, fulltime equivalent student. The mix of the students is not that different. Berkeley is 70 percent undergraduates and 30 percent graduate students. San Jose State is 80 percent undergraduates and 20 percent graduate students. Obviously, more of the Berkeley students are in PhD programs, but we have adjusted for that. The student-faculty ratio is very different, even after adjustment. The student-faculty ratio at Berkeley is 15:1, already roughly twice the ratio at the elite private universities, including Columbia, Stanford, Princeton, and Harvard. In comparison, the ratio at San Jose State is 26:1.

Now, let's look at the budgets of the two institutions, after removing all government research dollars from their budgets to obtain a fairer comparison of educational costs. The Berkeley budget is more an estimate of how much they spend on the education mission. I summed tuition, the state's subsidy, and one-half of their investment and gift income (assuming the other half was for the research mission). The costs are going to be sufficiently different that these estimates have little effect on the overall conclusion. San Jose has no endowment income and very little gift income, so you can omit those factors. What then is the cost per student when you do this quick kind of analysis? At Berkeley, the estimate is $26,800 per year. At San Jose State, it is $11,800 per year. My conclusion is that the cost of education in a research-intensive university is considerably higher; in fact, it appears that the ratio of costs exceeds even the differential student-faculty ratio. This difference in costs may be due to a variety of factors, from higher faculty salaries to smaller class sizes.

Now if you were to apply this analysis to other institutions, you would find the cost per student was much more varied. Berkeley may be more toward the high end and certainly has a track record of accomplishment that justifies the investment. But then, only a few research universities are of Berkeley's caliber. I think we have to accept that nationally we may not be able to afford as many research institutions going forward as we have had, unless we can find alternative sources of funding. I do not think such funding is likely to come from the federal government, or from state government. The only place it is going to come from is a significant growth in philanthropy going to those institutions. This is an important issue for the country.

## Is the Real Crisis Cost, or Is It Completion?

Getting back to Professor Bowen's question, which came near the end of his lecture, we must ask ourselves: Do we have a crisis? I think we definitely have a cost problem, but I believe that our true crisis is not around costs but around college completion. If you look at completion rates, let us just put them in rough numbers. The public universities have completion rates of around 55 percent in six years for full-time incoming freshmen. (Given leaves, access to classes, and changes of majors, the six-year figure is probably appropriate.) For the private institutions, this number is just over 60 percent, and for four-year for-profits, the number is around 25 percent. These percentages are for students who start full-time. They ignore transfer students; adding students who transfer and complete adds as much as 10 percent to these graduation rates.

Now I propose that somebody should do an analysis I have never seen. Professor Bowen pointed out, in response to a question yesterday, the very positive return on investment accrued by somebody who completes a college degree. What is the return on investment for a student who does not complete a degree, if we include both college costs and the opportunity cost (incurred because the student isn't working)? If we did that analysis, I think we would find a rather different number, one that would cause us to focus much more on completion. It is one thing for a student to finish a degree and come out with $25,000 of debt (the average incurred in 2011); it is another thing for a student to go to college and walk away with $10,000–$15,000 of debt and no degree to show for it. A number of studies have shown that the difference between completion and non-completion in terms of economic outcomes is very large. Students may certainly derive benefits from being in college, but for those who do not graduate it is hard to demonstrate the clear economic advantages associated with completing a degree.

## Loan Burdens and Defaults

The issue of student indebtedness and loan defaults blends the challenges of cost and completion. Increasing costs drive up loan indebtedness, and lack of completion leads to lower financial rewards and greater probability of default. Recent data show that the default rate on student loans is going up very slowly for the nonprofits, but it is soaring in the for-profit institutions: from FY 2006–07 to FY 2008–09, in a period of only two years, the for-profit default rate went from 9.8 percent to 15.4 percent. Students who do not graduate default on their loans at much higher rates, which is exactly what you could expect. This combination is a growing crisis, partly related to the cost of higher education. The mediocre completion rates, however, remind us that achieving lower costs by measures that decrease completion rates would be a bad trade-off.

Can we tame the problem of growing costs without damaging completion rates? I think we probably can at least moderate it. I do wonder whether or not the higher education community has the willingness and courage to face up to the problem proactively or whether they will simply react in incremental steps. For example, budgets fall because either states or parents reduce what they pay; then we decide to cut departments or cut programs instead of thinking about how we might move forward in a different way. There are things you could do. For example, you could raise student-faculty ratios, which could directly improve productivity, but I think we would all agree it would reduce quality and possibly endanger completion rates. Increasing the ratio would clearly improve productivity according to traditional measures. I suspect that higher education parallels the information-technology paradox mentioned by Professor Bowen. Increasing the student-faculty ratio is just one of many things that would reduce cost but would probably also reduce the quality of the experience. Measuring that quality loss is very difficult. I think many of the points raised by Professors Gardner and Delbanco had to do with the quality of the experience and what students learn from that entire experience; this is not something easily measured by student-faculty ratios or by standardized tests.

This afternoon, Professor Bowen will advance a hypothesis that I am absolutely willing to entertain, if perhaps not fully ready to endorse yet: that technology may be our best answer to the question of how we can reduce cost while preserving what we do that is unique and excellent in our universities.

# William G. Bowen's Responses to Discussion Session Comments by Howard Gardner and John Hennessy

THERE IS SO much here that I cannot possibly respond to everything that has been said. Let me first offer a few comments that may be controversial and challenge some of our accepted thinking—including some of my own. The first observation I would make cuts across the two sets of remarks by our commentators. It concerns the stratification issue in higher education.

The difference in circumstances between Harvard, Yale, Stanford, Princeton—the top-tier places in terms of wealth—and everybody else is dramatic, and so it is not surprising to hear what John reported about Stanford's ability to provide more money to students who really need it, and more services for the students who really need them. The same thing is true at Princeton. It cannot be true at more than five or six places, maybe ten; and this tiny number of institutions together educates a very, very small fraction of the student population. Much more research needs to be done on both the extent of stratification (measured in many ways, not just in terms of money), and what all of this is going to mean over time. This is, I think, a big question.

Much as I would like to see more of the wonderful features of residential life that Howard described so well, and so very eloquently, it is by no means obvious that the resources are going to be there to make this possible—except in the wealthiest sector of higher education. One of the things that I am going to say this afternoon, in my second Tanner lecture, is that it is going to be crucially important to develop skillfully defined mixes of teaching methods that use online technologies to complement the best features of face-to-face interaction. But that is going to require considerable changes in decision-making models and in how we think about who in the academy should make what kinds of decisions. The models we have across the country for governance are models that are fifty, seventy-five years old, and whether they make sense in the digital age is an important question. I have my doubts.

I have my own recollections of the glories of wonderful student-teacher interactions, and of how much I benefited from them. Yet my good friend, William Baumol, who is smarter than essentially everybody, keeps reminding me that teachers are no different than doctors in that they tend to exaggerate their importance. They believe that, whether it is the bedside manner of the doctor or whether it is the twinkle in the eye of the engaging faculty member, they change lives profoundly; however, in most instances, this is very much an open question. As we think about the transition to sophisticated kinds of online teaching, we do well not to be too quick to accept what we want to believe about our own talents and their consequences.

The next point I would make has to do, Howard, with something else you said with which I agree—namely, that we should stop doing so much pandering to student taste of one kind or another. I am glad, John, that you are not proposing that at Stanford. That is good. But there is an important consequence which I am not sure very many universities and colleges either understand or are willing to accept—namely, that if you restrain yourself in this way, you are going to lose some students. My response: so what? I cannot tell you how many times at Princeton I met with admissions people who wanted to talk about yield. I said "Please, please, I do not want to hear one word about yield. I do not care what the yield is. What I care about is the quality of the students that we end up with in the fall. The fact that some number of other students to whom we offered admission chose, rightly or wrongly, wisely or unwisely, to go somewhere else is just fine—no issue for me. It does not make any difference." The pool of excellent candidates at places like Princeton is so deep that it is unimportant if the university loses a few of them on the margin. Of course, I recognize what a privileged place Princeton is, that the great majority of colleges and universities cannot be so cavalier about yield. But those that can be cavalier should be.

There is also a related point, which plagues the liberal arts colleges especially—namely, fear of rankings. It is even true that some presidents are, apparently, paid on the basis of the rankings. Lunatic! And the rankings are based far too heavily on SAT scores, which predict actually one thing very well: family wealth. They do not predict much else. Please go back and reread the relevant chapter in *Crossing the Finish Line*.

[*Audience comment*] Nothing predicts very well.

Well, that is not true. Your statement is an exaggeration. If you look at the *Crossing the Finish Line* book that my colleagues and I wrote not that long ago, you find a dramatic difference in the predictive power of achievement-based measures versus so-called aptitude tests. What matters is how students did in secondary school, and how they did on achievement tests, not how they did on the ACT or SAT. The differences in terms of predictive effects are dramatic. And when you stop and think about it, this is not really surprising. What does achievement-based performance measure? What does it tell you? It tells you who can get up off the floor after having been knocked down and do fine the next day. It tells you about coping skills. It tells you about motivation. It tells you about a whole set of things that really matter in terms of success both in college and in life. And yet, if places downplay the traditional aptitude-based, test-score measures of "quality," they pay a price in terms of rankings. My answer to the presidents with whom I discuss this is, "Fine. Let us hope that your board has brain enough to understand that rankings are not the currency in which things should be measured." So I think, Howard, that to move in the direction you suggest, places have to be willing to let the yield go where it will, to let the rankings go where they will, and to live with the consequences of focusing on the kind of education that we ought to provide—to put our resources where they are most needed.

Back to stratification. We need to distinguish very carefully between what is feasible at places with substantial resources and at places that do not have such wealth. When my colleagues and I were testing out a very sophisticated interactive statistics course developed by Carnegie Mellon, I asked someone who serves with me on the ITHAKA board, Steve Stigler, a world-famous statistician at the University of Chicago, to look at the statistics course and tell me, as an expert, what he thought of it. He said, "Well, you know, it is pretty good. But of course I teach differently, and better than that."

I said, "Steve, no question. If I have a choice between having a statistics course from you or having this machine-guided form of instruction, which am I going to choose? I am going to choose Steve Stigler in a heartbeat." But how many students have that choice? The choice for most people is not Steve Stigler versus machine-guided instruction; it is machine-guided instruction versus some unknown quality of instruction. Instructional quality is extremely varied. And so I think we need to be realistic in thinking about what the real choices are, and not glorify a Steve-Stigler option that is not real.

Finally, a word about collaboration. I believe in collaboration. It is, by and large, a good thing if it is handled wisely and in a tough-minded way. But there are dangers in collaboration. Absent efficient modes of decision-making, it is very hard to get good judgments made when nimbleness and truth telling are required. There can be too much politeness, too much inclination to say, "Oh, let me not force that answer on you, even though it is the right answer." And so too often we end up with lowest-common-denominator outcomes—with one participant in the collaboration insisting on this kind of a test which others know makes no sense. We go along. But it is very important in addressing some problems—not all, and there certainly are areas where collaboration works beautifully—not to be too collaborative. Let me cite athletics as an example. The membership decision-making models in athletics can be terrible. I participated in some of those for too long. It is the same cursed problem of wanting to be nice, of not wanting to offend.

# Discussion by Andrew Delbanco

GOOD MORNING. I want to add my thanks to everyone already mentioned and, indeed, to everyone involved with this series of lectures. Daphne and I talked over the plan for this morning's session, and we agreed that I should go first since there's some risk that I may sound a down note on which we wouldn't want to end. But perhaps it won't be quite as down as you might anticipate.

First, however, I want to add a more extended thanks to President Bowen not only for these very helpful lectures but also for his innumerable contributions that, for many years, have elevated the national conversation about higher education. He has made the case for race-conscious admissions not only as morally imperative but also as effective social policy. He has argued (to use his own formulation) for putting a "thumb on the scale" in the case of low-income students hoping to become the first in their family to attend a selective college. As he mentioned yesterday, he has made the case for favoring high school grades over standardized test scores as better predictors of college success. He has alerted us to the problem of undermatching and its negative effects on time-to-degree and graduation rates. And he has been frank about the corrosive effects of college athletics on academic values. That is, of course, only a partial list of Bill's interventions in the public debate. For all of these, we should be grateful. I hope we will also heed the warning he issued yesterday about the danger of accelerating stratification in higher education. This is something to which I will return in my comments.

I'd like to begin with a little exercise in iconography, focused on two images drawn from two recent magazine covers. I was excited about the idea of showing you PowerPoints because, as a resolutely low-tech type, I have never done that in a public talk. So there is perhaps some irony in the fact that when I came out here to Stanford—a leader in both the conceptualization and the implementation of technology—I was told that it would be simpler if I provided paper copies. In front of you, therefore, you should have a piece of paper with two color images. On the left, you see the cover of Tina Brown's latest editorial project, *Newsweek* magazine, which is, incidentally, about to cease paper publication (figure 6). We may have mixed feelings about Tina Brown's history as a media trendsetter, but it's hard to deny that she has been well attuned to public sentiment; and I think this picture captures quite well something that has been alluded to over the last couple of days, namely the public mood toward our colleges and universities. Consider the velvet lawn, which looks as if it could be the work of the greenskeepers at Augusta. Strolling across it is a solitary student couple (either they are late, or everyone else is still in bed) making their satiated way through Eden toward class, where, given the widespread fact of grade inflation, they seem likely to get a pair of As without too much exertion. It's an image that nicely captures the public perception of college as essentially an expensive dating service for pampered students. President Hennessy was quite convincing yesterday morning that this picture is in fact a gross caricature of the lives of most students, and he was persuasive, at least to me, that the proverbial climbing wall in the dorm and the café in the library

**Figure 6** *Newsweek* cover, September 11, 2012

THE NAZI DEATH CAMPS & THALIDOMIDE

SEPTEMBER 17, 2012

# Newsweek

## Is College a Lousy Investment?

By Megan McArdle

JOHN ROBERTS HATES SURPRISES
BY DANIEL KLAIDMAN

WHAT'S THE MATTER WITH NAOMI WOLF?
BY MICHELLE GOLDBERG

are not very significant drivers of college costs—at least not compared to some of the other factors that we have been discussing. The truth is that many, if not most, American undergraduates experience nothing like what's illustrated on this magazine cover. Something more than a third attend underfunded, overcrowded community colleges with few amenities and certainly no luxuries; and a growing portion of those students are adults with jobs and families that leave them little time for anything but work and more work. Yet however much it may be at odds with reality, this picture does capture the widespread perception of college as a wasteful indulgence—a perception which, as Bill rightly said in his first lecture, undermines public support and could eventually endanger every aspect of higher education from Pell grants for needy students to NIH funding for research scientists.

Now let me show you a second image, which speaks to the theme of President Bowen's second lecture. Could there be a technological fix for the twin problems of college costs and weak learning outcomes? Here, the iconography gets a little more complicated (figure 7). We have a young man who appears to be Asian, or perhaps Eurasian. Either way he represents a kind of benign convergence of cultures that are sometimes seen as in competition or conflict with one another. He is a good globalist. He consumes American products. (Note the Apple logo on his laptop.) He is left-handed, which signifies, at least to left-handers, that he is exceptionally gifted. He is disciplined: you notice that he's eating a healthy breakfast, some sort of high-fiber cereal sprinkled with fruit, very different from the high–sugar and carb breakfast I ate this morning; and he is studying on a schedule dictated by his own biorhythms rather than by some arbitrary classroom schedule. He is a good student, or at least he aspires to be. (Note the Stanford-of-the-East logo on his coffee mug.) And, as suggested by that reassuring symbol of domesticity, the dog sleeping at his feet, he poses no threat to traditional American values. You could push this analysis even a little further and note that he is sitting at a folding movable table that's been interposed between two heavy old-fashioned tables—a suggestion, perhaps, that some heavy lifting was required in order to create the new online educational space that he now occupies. Yet to my eye, the most striking thing about this picture is that the young man is *alone*. Any connection he has to his peers is, as we say today, a virtual one; and it should also be noted that he inhabits the same space where he goes shopping, socializes, seeks entertainment, and, if he's at all representative of many computer users, sneaks a peek at pornography now and then.

**Figure 7** *Boston* magazine cover, September 2012

THE EDUCATION ISSUE

# THE 50 BEST PUBLIC HIGH SCHOOLS
OUR EXCLUSIVE RANKING

# Boston

## IS THIS THE COLLEGE CLASSROOM OF THE FUTURE?

HOW FREE ONLINE COURSES FROM HARVARD & MIT ARE REVOLUTIONIZING WHAT IT MEANS TO GO TO COLLEGE

PLUS

ON THE CAMPAIGN TRAIL WITH SCOTT BROWN & ELIZABETH WARREN

FALL FASHION: BOLD LOOKS FOR A CRISP NEW SEASON

bostonmagazine.com   $4.99us.
09 >

Our question over the last two days has been whether this second image holds promise to remedy the problems implicit in the first. The first thing I want to say is that there have been others before us who think the answer to that question is yes. I stumbled recently on a report issued some fifty years ago by the Ford Foundation on the potential of new technology for improving higher education. At that time, the new technology in question was television. Its potentialities seemed much like those of the Internet today: "This new technology," the authors wrote, "would extend the reach of the superior teacher to greater numbers of students," and would "improve and extend the quality of teaching" by relieving the professor of the "semester to semester parroting of himself." In other words, we have here an early version of what today is called the flipped classroom. The idea was that introductory instruction—drudgery for the teacher and duty for the student—could be delivered over the airwaves by an especially talented lecturer, allowing the face-to-face classroom to be reserved for higher-order activities. And not least among its promises, according to that report, the new technology promised to save institutions from the spiraling cost cycle that was already felt to be a problem in the early 1960s.

Now, the explanation of why none of these things happened will seem obvious enough: the technology back then was simply not up to the task. By comparison to what we have today, television was rudimentary and primitive. It did not allow for interaction between teacher and student, or for what I like to call lateral learning—dialogue between student and student. We hear the same explanation today for the failure of some early attempts to harness the Internet as a force for transforming higher education. At my own university, for instance, there was an effort some fifteen years ago to start a company called Fathom.com—an online enterprise from which Columbia hoped to earn money that would help close the gap between our financial resources and those of our better-endowed competitors. After that effort collapsed, one of Bill Bowen's collaborators, a young Columbia alumna named Taylor Walsh, examined what had happened in a valuable book entitled *Unlocking the Gates: How and Why Leading Universities are Opening Up Access to Their Courses* (2011). In that book, she quotes an explanation for the failure of Fathom from one of the project leaders: "We were pre broadband, pre video casting and iPods and all the rest." Now, to my mind, the trouble with such an explanation is that we will always be pre-something. The real question today is whether, after many false starts, we have finally acquired the power to realize the deferred dream of transforming the quality of, and access to, higher education via technology. Bill Bowen himself has gone from skepticism, as expressed in his Romanes Lecture delivered at Oxford twelve years ago, to the cautious optimism we heard from him yesterday evening that the new technologies may hold promise for ameliorating, if not eradicating, the "cost disease" that has long plagued our colleges and universities.

The famous Baumol-Bowen theory about the etiology of that disease makes an analogy between professors and musicians—a comparison to which Bill alluded in his first lecture on Wednesday evening. Four string players, he reminded us, require as much time to play a Beethoven quartet today as would have been required in the nineteenth century, when the piece was first composed and performed. Like teaching and learning, music making is not an area of human endeavor where one can speak intelligibly about advances in efficiency or productivity. It's not clear what such an advance might mean.

Yet in listening to Bill, I was reminded of something I heard from one of my high school science teachers back around 1968—a prediction that seemed fanciful and fantastic even at that time of big dreams. This teacher (who was also a good musician) said, "Look, it won't be long before you won't need to travel to Carnegie Hall and pay to hear some future Heifetz or Oistrakh play the Beethoven violin concerto." He was making that claim early in the computer age, when no one had yet heard of a PC, much less a tablet or smartphone. Yet he was confident that sooner or later we would have a relatively cheap technology that could reproduce the sound of the greatest instruments as played by the greatest musicians. The whole notion of in-person virtuoso performance would become obsolete, and we would get the Carnegie Hall experience—minus the cost and the coughing—in our own homes. We're not quite there yet, but we're certainly a lot closer than we were when my teacher made that prediction forty-five years ago.

To return to the sphere of education, let us assume that we have indeed arrived at a moment when it's at least plausible to imagine some version of the technological fix—that we will have a new tool for ameliorating, if not curing, the chronic disease of high cost and low efficiency. The future may not be quite at hand, but it may be close enough to allow at least a glimpse of what it will bring and what it will mean. President Hennessy tells us that when it arrives, it will have the force of a tsunami. That's an interesting metaphor, since, as far as I know, the effects of tsunamis are highly destructive. It's a metaphor in keeping with what one advocate of the online movement, the Harvard Business School professor Clayton Christensen, calls "disruptive innovation"—a variant of Joseph Schumpeter's famous description of capitalism as a continual process of "creative destruction." In light of such predictions, it would seem that one question we should be asking ourselves is, what will be disrupted or destroyed, and what will be innovated or created?

If we can disrupt, even if not destroy, the cost disease, that would be terrific. If we can destroy obstacles to educational attainment of the sort that Bill has enumerated, that would be great. I am impressed by the serious engagement of many faculty, some of them here in this room, who are trying to deploy these new technologies toward those ends. I also sense in them a sincere conviction that technology may lead us to understand better how students learn and that it can be deployed not only to create a new kind of educational experience but, through "hybrid" or "blended" forms, it can make the traditional kind better. I am convinced that Daphne and her colleagues have ideals as big as their dreams, which became clear to me the other night at dinner when I had the pleasure of sitting across from Daphne—an experience that I'm tempted to describe as classic face-to-face learning.

At the same time, to consider a little longer President Hennessy's metaphor, it seems to me we ought to acknowledge that tsunamis are not exactly known for their selectivity. They do not pick and choose what they wash away. So I want to make two points about what else, besides the cost disease, may be in danger of disruption or destruction.

First, let me say something that may be screamingly obvious: the faculty as we have known it is at risk. I think we should be candid about the severity and imminence of the risk. In responding to a question at yesterday morning's session, President Hennessy rightly asserted that we must get used to the idea that faculties will shrink as technologies grow. Some months ago, at a gathering somewhat similar to this one, I heard an even blunter assessment from Paul LeBlanc, president of the University of Southern New Hampshire—an institution that has moved strongly into online education—who said that the new technologies pose to faculty nothing less than an "existential threat."

I think he was right. For one thing, there is the prospect that the new technologies will greatly increase stratification, not only among institutions but also among faculty members within institutions. There is also large potential for accelerating the movement of faculty toward extrainstitutional affiliations and loyalties—a process that has been under way since the professionalization of the academic disciplines in the late nineteenth century, when faculty began to think of themselves less as members of a local college or university community and more as geographically scattered professionals whose first loyalty was to their shared discipline. In many ways, this development in faculty culture was a good thing. It reduced provincialism, dilettantism, and institutional inbreeding. But it also planted the seeds of today's star system—creating opportunities for the absentee professor, the "Logan" rather than "local" professor to whom Howard Gardner alluded yesterday. By the mid-twentieth century, this process was well along, and Clark Kerr was describing the Berkeley faculty as "individual entrepreneurs held together by a common grievance over parking." By the late twentieth century, Henry Rosovsky, the long-serving dean of the Faculty of Arts and Sciences at Harvard, was accusing the Harvard faculty of making "its own rules" with regard to teaching loads, outside business ventures, consulting time versus teaching time, and so on.

I suspect that the new technologies have considerable potential for strengthening these centrifugal forces that drive faculty away from their home institutions. Star faculty with a web presence will command large speaking fees and will have more and more incentive to spend time on the road (actual as well as virtual) because people will always pay to see celebrities in person. Just last night, a lot of people in Brooklyn paid $350 per person to hear and see Barbra Streisand in the flesh despite the fact that she sounds better on the CDs she made thirty years ago than she does in person today. Though minimal by comparison, similar opportunities (or temptations, depending on how you look at them) are already available to academics. One Day University, for instance, a low-tech enterprise in which I have participated myself, charges admission to a few hundred adults who pay to attend lectures by college professors, who receive, in return, a not-negligible fee.

It's safe to predict, I think, that for some faculty, opportunities of this sort will grow with the expansion of online education, while others—whose star power may be smaller but whose intellectual power may be as large or larger—will be consigned to second-class status simply because they teach an arcane or difficult subject with less public appeal. For still others—language faculty, for instance—there's a prospect not only of diminished status but also of obsolescence. The French teacher of the future may be a French-speaking version of Siri on your iPhone. If I am right about these trends, we should be worried about the persistence of academic community in anything more than the nominal sense.

Now, Bill has spoken of the urgent need for reconsidering the structures of academic governance to enable institutions to grapple with these and many other implications of the online revolution. Yet universities have so far done little to redefine conflict-of-interest principles to fit the new reality that is already upon us. If nothing is done, the already-fragile coherence of academic institutions will come under intense new pressure. On the other hand, if new definitions become too restricting, the most sought-after faculty will simply jump ship and go to work for themselves as freelance online celebrities. In some measure, it's already happening. Yet these prospects, along with many attendant questions, have so far failed to provoke much discussion inside or outside academia. Perhaps most important, we should ask how the training of future faculty should be carried on in this new context. What are the implications for aspiring academics? Will they spend years in graduate training in order to become glorified teaching assistants to a few media stars?

I want also to say that I'm a little surprised that our focus on the MOOCs over the last few days has not prompted much comment about the parallel rise of the for-profit entities that call themselves universities—enterprises such as Phoenix, DeVry, Strayer, and the rest. There has been mention of the role of for-profit "universities" in worsening the student loan problem, and Bill has always expressed caution about the implications of profit-seeking in academia, as when he spoke, in his Romanes Lecture, about "the limits of markets as definers of values and allocators of resources." Yet as we all know, a lot of smart people are betting on the profit potential of the new technologies that are taking hold within and around academic institutions. As time goes on, it seems inevitable that we will witness a merging of cultures between traditional nonprofit institutions and the rising for-profit sector—a merger in which there is surely risk of loss as well as gain.

Of course, if either the promise or peril of the new technologies is to be realized, significant revenues will have to be found, and no one seems yet to know where these revenues will come from. They may come from charging fees for certification, through in-person supplementary experiences, by providing screening services for potential employers, or contracting with textbook publishers, or some combination of such strategies—as well as, no doubt, many more. Whatever the future holds, I worry that it won't be a simple matter to retain the high-mindedness that characterizes the best of today's pioneers of Internet learning.

My second point is about the promise or peril of the new technology for students themselves. In that mid-twentieth-century report on the educational promise of television to which I have alluded, we find the key question: "How effective is this instruction?" The technology has changed, but the question ought not to change. Yesterday, Bill gave us a provisionally positive answer based, in part, on a careful study of the Carnegie Mellon Open Learning Initiative. I take encouragement from that study, but I think we would all agree that many questions remain about who learns what and how much—especially from the rapidly proliferating MOOCs. How can we apply traditional measures such as retention or completion rates to these new educational "delivery systems"? And if we can't, how can we assess their educational value alongside their revenue-producing value?

Moreover, even as we look for new ways to answer this imperative question—"How effective is this instruction?"—I feel the need to demur from the terms in which it is formulated. My demurral concerns the word *instruction*, which takes me back a few weeks to a class in which I was discussing the writings of Ralph Waldo Emerson with my undergraduates at Columbia. At one point, I called to their attention a statement Emerson made to the graduating class of the Harvard Divinity

School in 1838. "Strictly speaking," he told those aspiring ministers, "it is not instruction, but provocation that I receive from another soul."

For me, at least, Emerson's point brings sharply into view the question of how online education can, or can't, serve those fields of learning that we customarily call the humanities. In this matter, I don't think it is possible to overemphasize the distinction between instruction and provocation. It's a distinction that can be restated in many ways: facts versus knowledge; skill versus wisdom; discipline versus inspiration; information versus insight. Thoughtful writers on education have explored these distinctions for many centuries. The categories of instruction and provocation are certainly not mutually exclusive, or even oppositional, but neither are they identical; and I think we can agree that a true education in any field—scientific as much as humanistic—entails both. Moreover, whichever terms we prefer, it seems uncontroversial to assert that education in the United States, not just in higher education but also K–12 education, has been moving lately toward the first term in the pair and away from the second. I believe that the online technologies are likely to move the needle further and faster in that direction.

Let me try to be concrete about this point, at risk of being mawkishly personal. If I am asked to illustrate what a real teacher-student exchange can mean, I think back to a moment in a seminar I took early in my years as a graduate student working in the field of early American literature. I was very fortunate to encounter at that time a great teacher who had noticed that I was putting up resistance to the predestinarian doctrines of the Calvinist theologian Jonathan Edwards, whom we were studying. I did not like Edwards's determinism (although as I speak to you this morning, it occurs to me that there's more than a little determinist flavor in my own remarks), and toward the end of the semester, this teacher turned to me and said, "What is it exactly that bothers you about Edwards? Could it be that he is so hard on self-deception?" Now, here was a teacher who had been paying attention to what I had been saying, thinking, and writing in the course of the seminar, who had a real sense of who I was, or, as the phrase goes, where I was coming from. The question he asked me has stayed with me ever since. Maybe it will be possible to preserve that kind of experience in the "flipped classroom" of the future. I hope so.

A lot of people seem to think so. David Brooks had a column not long ago saying that technology will enable us to clear more space for this kind of encounter—for provocation—by relegating instruction to the online platform where it can be provided more efficiently and economically. But I am not convinced.

I'm not convinced in part because it makes little sense to me to organize our teaching in the humanities into the categories of "introductory" and "advanced." There is, of course, a certain sense in which humanistic learning is sequential (one needs to know Shakespeare, for example, to hear the Shakespearean echoes in Melville), but this is true to a much smaller degree than in the sciences. In the humanities, description is also and always interpretation. But the key point here, which Bill touched on poignantly toward the end of his lecture yesterday, is that the humanities have to do not only with cognition and comprehension, but with *values*. You will recall that story he told about the ten-year-old Jeff Bezos proudly informing his grandmother of how much she was shortening her life by smoking cigarettes, and his grandfather saying to him, "Someday you will realize that it's harder to be kind than to be clever." My question is, can we preserve an educational environment where teaching kindness as well as cleverness is a serious part of our collective aspiration? Can online instruction foster that kind of teaching? Let's hope so.

I am going to ask for your indulgence just a little longer because I want to read a portion of an e-mail that one of my teaching assistants received last week after he had led a discussion about the same writer I mentioned earlier, namely Emerson. Here is the e-mail:

> Hi, I just wanted to let you know that our section meeting tonight had a really profound effect on me. I scribbled down four pages worth of thoughts and my copy of the book is probably unreadable through all my comments in it, but the way you spoke and the energy our class had really moved me. I am not usually one to feel things, especially deep existential emotions, but tonight I feel connected to the text and I owe a lot of that to you. I walked the whole way home staring at the sky, a probably unsafe decision but a worthwhile one nonetheless. I actually cannot wait for next week's class so I can dive further into this. I just wanted to send you a quick message, thanking you, letting you know that this 50 minutes of class has affected the rest of my life. Sorry if that is weird but some fire was lit within me tonight and I guess I am blowing the smoke towards you a little bit.

I am sure everybody in this room agrees that we want to do everything we can to preserve the kind of experience this student describes, so that it will be available in the future not just to privileged students attending institutions where person-to-person teaching remains affordable but to as many students as possible. The online future is rapidly approaching and, in some respects, is already here. I only hope that when we look back at the superseded past, we will not say, as Emerson's friend Henry David Thoreau said about an earlier technological revolution, "We do not ride upon the railroad, the railroad rides upon us." Thank you.

# Discussion by Daphne Koller

**GOOD MORNING.** That will be a very tough act to follow. I am going to try to respond to a few, not all, of Professor Delbanco's points in the comments that I will make, and hopefully, we will tackle some of the rest in the discussion. Let me begin at a very similar point to Professor Delbanco's talk. Professor Bowen started his second talk saying that he was initially skeptical about the value of online learning but has come to believe that perhaps now is the time when this technology will actually come to fruition and help us come up with a transformed educational experience. A question that I get asked often is what is it that makes this different from the multiple previous attempts, the multiple notorious failures—such as the Fathom project—that did not succeed in transforming the shape of education. Here we can also include the TV-based efforts, which I was not even aware of because they long predate me. There are a lot of little pieces which I'll come to in a moment, but if you had to put your finger on one thing, it is the recognition that this new form of teaching is really a new educational paradigm. That is, it is not and should not be taking in-class instruction and trying to replicate it in an online medium.

By thinking about this in a completely new way, we can release ourselves from the shackles that we have gotten used to in the context of in-class teaching. And, while perhaps losing some of the benefits of face-to-face instruction, we can gain in other ways. By contrast, in the other approach you lose some of the benefits of in-class instruction without gaining anything, or very little. I think that this realization has led to a lot of the specific innovations that have really contributed to the success that we have seen in this new generation of online learning platforms, ours as well as others in this space. Perhaps most important, there's the fact that interaction of at least two different types needs to be built into the learning process.

First, there is interaction of the student with the material. We should avoid a passive one-way communication where the students are sitting there with the information flowing unidirectionally toward them, as was the case in the TV-based or in the Fathom effort. Rather, we should aim for a constant interaction with the computer, which is now capable of "talking back" to the students.

Equally or perhaps even more important is the fact that students can actually rub minds with each other via the computer. Now, this is something that to the people of my generation is still a little bit foreign, but if you talk to the kids of today, the eighteen-year-olds, they actually prefer to text each other rather than to talk to each other on the phone or even get together for coffee. That kind of interaction via an electronic medium is something that is really built into the culture now. It has been built into us by Facebook, by Twitter, by text messaging. An important lesson from this generation of students is that we should not presume, because of the way that we were brought up, that rubbing minds can only happen in face-to-face interaction. The rubbing of minds via digital media is a key to the success of this new generation of teaching platforms. Many of our students who have taken some of the courses on the platform tell us that in fact, this is a far more interactive experience than they have ever had in face-to-face instruction.

Now, this is not the case, I am sure, for Professor Delbanco's ten-person seminar, which is a truly unique experience that any of us would be privileged to participate in. But consider most of the kids in large universities, who are shoveled into large auditoriums with three hundred people and the professor standing down there and lecturing at them. And then they go off to their dorm rooms and do their homework. These kids get a lot more interaction with both the material and their fellow students by being on this online system where they interact with each other on a constant basis. If I had known that we were going to hear this very inspiring quote from Professor Delbanco at the end of his talk, I could have given multiple similar quotes from many of our tens of thousands of students. In particular, I could probably have come up with hundreds from our class of 33,000 students who are taking Al Filreis's Modern and Contemporary American Poetry class. Al Filreis is the head of the U. Penn Writing Center. His typical class there is a small seminar, much like Professor Delbanco's. But he has 33,000 students in his online class. And he gets e-mails from students that are very similar to what we just heard, about how these interactions have opened these students' minds to a new way of looking at poetry, have allowed them to interact with their peers in a way that is centered on the course material but also transcends geographical boundaries, and have provided them with really profound communication with large groups of people that they would never, in the ordinary course of events, have the opportunity to meet.

I wanted to start off with that comment because I think it is important to respond to some of the justified caution in the notes that we have heard. In particular, it is important not to come in with too strong of a set of preconceptions about what online technology can and cannot do in terms of rubbing minds and in terms of inspiring groups of people who would never have the opportunity of taking Professor Delbanco's class.

With that said, I am going to switch to a different topic, which follows on one of the most important observations made at the very start of Professor Bowen's first lecture, the key metric of productivity. That is, the ratio of outputs relative to inputs or outcomes relative to costs. Now, as Professor Bowen eloquently argues, in the context of education, we cannot actually measure either the numerator or the denominator; in fact, we do not even know what we are measuring, which clearly limits our ability to measure productivity and try to improve it. This is one place, among many, where Professor Bowen was a true leader in the field; he was the first to highlight the notion of completions rather than enrollments as a key measure of productivity. He also focused on learning outcomes as being a key measure of productivity: the understanding of the material as well as the ability to use the material in new and innovative ways. And then, if we want to move beyond that, there are also longer-term outcomes, such as the ability of a student graduating with a degree to earn a good living and, even more important, to have high job satisfaction. That is, we want our graduating students to be proud of what they do when they go to work every day. All of these, of course, are even harder to measure than the costs.

On my optimistic days, I would argue that one of the great promises of technology in education is that if done right—and I think that qualifier is important—it can enact significant change for the better in both the numerator and the denominator of this equation. I would like to talk about each of those pieces. Let me start with one of the key aspects of the second talk, which is the seminal ITHAKA study on the gains of online methodologies and improving efficiencies within academic institutions. This was a landmark study because it was the first rigorous case-control study that actually compared learning outcomes between blended and face-to-face learning. And certainly there were a lot of promising aspects of that study. The first is to demonstrate conclusively (although I will come back to that) that there was no difference in learning outcomes in these two populations. That means that the numerator was left unchanged, and the denominator was potentially improved in at least two ways. First was a decrease of 25 percent in the amount of time spent by students, so that was an improvement in the cost, at least the cost to the students. Second, to a certain extent, there was an analysis suggesting that we could achieve a reduction in the investment required by the institution in terms of instructor and TA effort.

The reductions, however, were relatively modest, and it seems like no matter how optimistic we are going to be, we are likely to see a reduction in costs of on-campus instruction by a factor of about two or three at best. Of course, as Professor Bowen correctly points out, it is hard to judge steady-state improvements in costs over a long time frame from a single instance because obviously, efficiency will improve as we learn to do blended learning better. But still, there are many reasons to be concerned about potential lack of reductions in costs, whether because of the caps on section sizes or because of the need, whether real or perceived, by instructors at institutions to customize the curriculum for their own students. And, therefore, if there is going to be productivity improvement in academic institutions, maybe it is not going to be in the denominator.

And so where is the potential in improving productivity in this process? I would argue that perhaps it comes in the numerator. This comes back to what is, to me, one of the disappointing aspects of the study, which is that there is no difference in learning outcomes. Blended learning was not better than face-to-face instruction. Now, some of you might be sitting there saying, why would you expect it to be any better? After all, common wisdom has it that it is only going to hurt our students to move to an online format, so why would you be disappointed by something that showed no change? For me, there are two arguments as to why blended learning might be better, although, obviously, these remain to be proven.

The first comes back to the beginning of my comments, in which I argue that the current online format is actually considerably different from many other online attempts in the past and is considerably more interactive and engaging than a standard lecture. Not more engaging than sitting in a seminar of ten or fifteen people, but when compared to the three-hundred-person auditorium, it actually is a much more interactive experience for the students. There is an incredible amount of educational research by renowned experts in the field that shows that this type of interaction and adaptation lead to better learning outcomes. Some improvements arise from the fact that students are constantly tested on the material. Others arise from the ability to enforce mastery in a given topic before the students move on to the next. These are strategies that online methodologies can help us implement but perhaps were not employed to their fullest extent in our attempts up to now.

The second reason for hope is that moving lecturing out of the classroom supports active learning in the classroom—the ability for an instructor to engage in meaningful ways with the students and for students to engage in meaningful ways with the other students. Now, this particular ITHAKA study did not demonstrate that the blended-learning format gave rise to that type of improvement. However, there are many studies by Eric Mazur, Carl Wieman, and others that have demonstrated significant gains to active learning in the classroom. So why did these benefits not manifest here? One answer is that, for some reason, they don't arise in a blended-learning format, even if they do when students are asked to read material outside the class. That answer doesn't seem all that plausible. A second argument draws on Professor Bowen's own argument, and I am going to quote: "A fundamental problem, cutting across all types of online offerings, is that contemporaneous comparisons of the costs of traditional modes of teaching and of newly instituted online pedagogies are nearly useless in projecting steady-state savings—or, worse yet, highly misleading. The reason is that the costs of doing almost anything for the first time are very different from the costs of doing the same thing numerous times." This was an argument as to why we did not see significant improvements in the costs; but maybe it is also the reason why we did not see significant improvements in learning outcomes. Because I can tell you, as someone who has flipped my own classroom for three years now, promoting active learning in the classroom is *hard*. It is not the kind of thing that we were trained to do. We were trained to stand and orate, and if you have been doing it, like I have, for over fifteen years, you tend to become reasonably good at it. Whereas the kind of pedagogy that is required for active learning in the classroom is considerably different. And until you learn that skill, you might not see the better learning outcomes that we hope to see from this new pedagogical intervention of blended learning. So perhaps the fact that we did not see an improvement is not because it could not exist but because, like potential cost reductions, it does not exist yet. This, I think, is one of the most exciting opportunities here.

The second aspect of why I think there is a potential here for significant improvements is the issue of capacity and completion. This is an issue that was briefly mentioned, whereby many community colleges are currently running up against serious capacity constraints. Indeed, in one of the many interesting endnotes to his talk, Professor Bowen points out that a survey by the California community college system shows that as of this summer, more than 472,000 of the system's 2.4 million students were put on waiting lists for core classes, meaning that they could not make the required progress toward their degree. Enrollment in the California community college system has decreased by close to 500,000 students due to budget cuts, and the number of course sections has been reduced by 24 percent. These reductions give rise to a significant increase in time to completion and presumably also a decrease in completion rates, as people just get tired of waiting around to be admitted into the classes they need in order to complete their degree.

Online learning, by allowing us to increase section sizes and reduce instructor teaching loads, might allow us to increase capacity at community colleges and other institutions, which would allow us to improve, again, the numerator: both increasing completions and reducing completion time to six or maybe, who knows, even four years.

The third potential for improvements is in long-term outcomes, which I briefly alluded to earlier. These online courses have the potential of allowing community colleges as well as other small schools to expand their curricula beyond the expertise and resource constraints of their current instructional staff. They can draw upon courses from Princeton or Stanford or Columbia and offer those to their own students with some additional on-site enhancements, such as blended learning. This expansion would allow students who are attending these institutions to add to their transcripts courses that might make them more eligible for better jobs. For example, in my own discipline, a course in machine learning is an excellent addition to a student's transcript and can easily make a student eligible for a job in some of the top IT companies. However, such a course can generally be offered only by the top twenty or thirty computer science departments, because of the difficulty of hiring instructors qualified to teach it. If we can offer this class in a much larger set of institutions, we can suddenly make a large number of students considerably more eligible for high-quality positions in companies such as Google or Twitter.

A fourth, even longer-term, opportunity is that of using data and analytics. This is an opportunity that we have yet to execute on, but one with huge potential. We can now collect every click from tens of thousands of students and start analyzing what in our classes is working and what is not: what our students are confused about, and when they figure it out, what they did to reach that understanding. That is something that is going to allow us to improve the way in which we teach our on-campus courses and again, this is not an advantage that you see the very first time that this is done.

A very different opportunity for improvement, one that was not really highlighted in Professor Bowen's talk, is the ability of these open online courses to be supportive of metrics of success in on-campus teaching even by students who are not enrolled in those institutions. Some of you might know that the Gates foundation put out a request for proposals a few weeks ago for MOOCs in twenty-seven of the highest-enrollment classes in the United States, a list that comprises developmental skills courses (math and English), some gateway classes, and basic general education classes. Those twenty-seven classes account for 20 percent of the units taken by students in the United States. If students could take these classes as MOOCs before they even enrolled in an academic institution, they would be able to come in with a significant number of units already under their belt. That could be a huge win in terms of increasing completion rates, because students who come in with a certain number of credits are much more likely to complete than ones who come in with a blank slate. This could also improve learning outcomes by having students come in considerably better prepared.

Another opportunity of open courses is that they allow the students a free exploration opportunity. People can take courses without financial cost and without risk of a failure on their transcript, which means that students can explore. They can take a little bit of psychology, a little bit of literature, a little bit of math and find out the right fit for them at zero risk before they enter an academic institution. They can also identify the level of challenge to which they can aspire, potentially reducing the mismatch problem that was also mentioned in Professor Bowen's talk. A student might say, "Hey, I can take and do well at a Stanford class, so maybe I should apply to Stanford after all." This, I think, is another opportunity for improvements.

Finally, I would like to talk about education outside the boundaries of academic institutions. This is a topic that Professor Bowen explicitly said he was not going to talk about, but I would like to talk about it for just a couple of minutes in conclusion. Education transcends the boundaries of our academic institutions. Most of the students currently taking these open online classes are educated professionals, often with one or more degrees. They want to take these courses sometimes to enhance their credentials for jobs but, in many other cases, just to expand their minds. The people taking modern poetry are probably not doing it to get a better job. We see in these courses a testament to the value of education across the range of disciplines. This observation comes back to one of the points that was made very early in the talk, that of booster shots of education. We no longer live in a world where what we were taught in college twenty years ago is enough to last us for our entire life. The world now changes much too quickly. To continue to have access to the best jobs, or even just to stay informed as world citizens, these booster shots are going to play an important role.

Finally, our discussion so far has been very U.S.-centric. I am going to step outside the United States for a moment and think about the fact that currently two-thirds or more of the students taking these classes are not within the United States. That globalization of education has benefits to us even within the United States. The very fact that our students can interact with people in Kazakhstan and Bangladesh is a way of opening people's minds to a much more global perspective. Along those lines, Mitch Duneier, a Princeton professor who taught the first humanities MOOC, says that "within three weeks, I had received more feedback on my sociological ideas than I had in a career of teaching, which significantly influenced each of my subsequent lectures and seminars." He specifically speaks to the global perspective in stating that feedback from thousands of students around the world was fundamental to his perception of his teaching.

Another benefit to opening our doors up to the world is that, again from a selfish perspective, there is unique talent in Mongolia, in Ghana, in Bangladesh—students who achieve perfect scores in some of our most challenging courses. This gives us the opportunity to recruit and identify some of the world's best talent to come to our institutions and enhance our own talent pool and the mix of students that we teach.

But I would like to conclude with a more unselfish view. We are uniquely privileged in the world in having access to high-quality education. As an example, the average amount invested in the education of a U.S. child by the time they graduate is about $100,000. The average amount invested in the education of an African child is $400—lower by a factor of 250. If we could educate more people, that has the potential of making the world a much better place, because many of the world's problems can be alleviated by education, including hunger, unemployment, extremism, and even population explosion. One interesting statistic that I have recently seen is that there is a strong inverse correlation between the number of children a woman typically has in a country and the number of years of education for girls in that country. This pattern holds up even after one corrects for culture, for religion, for wealth. Education of women is a way of reducing the population explosion.

The value of education is something that is clearly recognized by some of the world's poorest people, who are the ones who can benefit the most. In September, I attended the launch of the Education First Initiative in the United Nations, and the former British prime minister Gordon Brown, who is now the special envoy for education at the United Nations, spoke of his travels in Africa. He spoke of talking with people who lived on a cup of food a day, but when asked what they want, they didn't say more food, they didn't say better shelter—what they most want is a better education for their children. And so, in our discussion of cost reductions, we shouldn't forget one place where costs are really important: in allowing us to reduce the marginal costs per student to the point that we can actually provide an education to people who otherwise would never be able to afford it.

# William G. Bowen's Responses to Discussion Session Comments by Andrew Delbanco and Daphne Koller

IT IS EVIDENT that Daphne is a true believer! And when I referred earlier to the missionary spirit, here you see it incarnate, and it is wonderful to see. What I think is especially admirable is that in Daphne, the missionary spirit is blended with an understanding that you do have to test things and to look for evidence. As I have said, a big barrier to greater acceptance of online learning is the lack of evidence concerning both learning outcomes and cost savings. Assembling evidence takes thought and it takes patience; it is also very, very important.

Let me now turn to Andy's remarks, which I thought were very good. Your comments, Andy, about the value of provocations remind me to underscore something that I may not have emphasized sufficiently. In our desire to experiment and to try new things, it is important to recognize that the pedagogy best suited to teaching in one field may not be the same pedagogy that is appropriate in a different field. A one-size-fits-all attitude is dangerous because it will lead both to bad teaching methods and to confusion about what is possible. I think there is merit in distinguishing, at least roughly, between fields in which there are understood facts or concepts that need to be acquired—and more discursive topics. What is a confidence interval? There is an answer to that question. That question is different in kind from discussion at a deep level of why the Palestinians and the Israelis have so much trouble getting together. Now that is a tremendously important question, but it is a very different question and requires a different way of thinking. We certainly need provocative teaching in subjects like that.

Now, I am not suggesting that we overdo this distinction; we should not. If you teach concepts well, you can generate a great deal of stimulating discussion, and I am impelled to mention a personal example. Without a doubt, the most powerful learning experience I ever had came when I was a frightened beginning graduate student in economics, taking William J. Baumol's course in economic theory. Professor Baumol used a book by J. R. Hicks called *Value and Capital,* probably one of the worst-written books ever produced, and I always suspected that Professor Baumol chose it in part for that reason. If I remember correctly, we covered in a semester-long course thirty-five pages. Thirty-five pages! Here is the way the course was taught. We would open the book and look at this incomprehensible, inscrutable paragraph, and Baumol would say, "All right, the assignment for next week is that each of you will go home and think, and write—write clearly—two pages explaining cogently what this paragraph actually means." I remember going back to my room and puzzling, puzzling, before going to bed—and all of a sudden waking up in the middle of the night and saying to myself: "I understand!" I then raced to my desk and wrote down what I thought was an insight before I lost it. What I learned from that experience was that I might not be as fast as others in the class in grasping every point, but, given time and persistence, I could actually figure many things out. I learned through that experience to have a kind of quiet confidence in what it was possible for me to achieve. That was a lesson of life, if you will, that was independent of the content. Particularly at advanced levels, we have to have the time, opportunity, and resources needed to permit that kind of life-changing experience—which is, to be sure, more likely to be provided by truly brilliant teachers such as Professor Baumol than by mere mortals.

Now, Baumol's approach did not work for everybody. I remember a classmate in that same course who, when asked to go to the blackboard (as Baumol always asked students to do), to take a piece of chalk, to draw a demand curve, and then to explain in a simple sentence what a demand curve is, was paralyzed. He finally just left the course and left economics forever—which was probably a good outcome all around. This is only to say, again, that we have to avoid all-or-nothing mindsets. How you teach statistics is different from the way you teach Melville. It *should* be different, and how you teach one set of students at one stage in their lives may be very different from how you teach others at different stages in their lives. This is why I argue for a portfolio approach to curricular development, for finding mixes of instructional styles, and mixes of pedagogies, that allow different kinds of learning to occur.

I should also take up a point that Daphne made with which I agree. In revising these lectures for publication, I will make clearer my sense that the equivalent learning outcomes we found in our empirical study of the CMU statistics course represent a kind of baseline. That is how these findings should be viewed. The teachers in the hybrid-online sections of the course we tested were inexperienced: they had never done anything like this before. Some of them seemed nearly baffled by the pedagogy. Some were essentially dragged, kicking and screaming, to this assignment. Could we do better? Certainly. Brit Kirwan, the enormously capable chancellor of the University System of Maryland, which was a participant in our project, is firmly convinced of that. Yes, learning outcomes will improve.

There were two big deficiencies in the very good CMU statistics course that we tested, both of which can be addressed. One was a lack of "fun." A friend of mine at CUNY explained the problem this way: "The course was just not fun. It was not addictive; it did not have any Disney-like features." Then there is the issue of customization, which is a tricky and complicated one. There is no doubt in my mind that a limitation of the course we tested was that it really could not be customized to meet "local" needs.

Let me mention another aspect of online teaching that, again, Daphne mentioned: adaptive learning. I have learned from Daphne how hard it is to incorporate truly adaptive learning in online courses. One of the great strengths of the Carnegie Mellon statistics course that we tested was that it was an adaptive learning course. If a student got something wrong, he or she could push a "hint" button and receive a well-thought-out suggestion as to how to do better. Such suggestions were based on evidence concerning the learning experiences of many students. If the student tried again and still got it wrong, pushing "hint" again would display another hint, and then another. When the student finally solved the problem, he or she was given another problem that was similar. That kind of machine-guided learning model works for certain content, probably not for Melville. It has great potential, especially in certain fields. But Daphne has helped me understand that this approach is really hard: it requires masses of data and discipline-specific knowledge. I think the pursuit of adaptive learning is on Coursera's radar screen, but it is down the road.

In terms of productivity, and numerators and denominators of productivity ratios, I intend in my revision of these lectures to do a better job of parsing out the elements of potential productivity gains. I agree that there is a huge potential for improving cost-effective learning outcomes by reducing time-to-degree and increasing completion rates. If, in fact, students can get through gateway courses faster, if they can present credentials that allow them to move through the system more rapidly, there could be substantial improvements in system-wide productivity.

I think in many ways the most challenging issue is one Andy identified: how to manage to keep the right value orientation and the real learning aspect of education in large, resource-strapped public universities. For many of these universities, the real challenge is how best to take some of the resources that can be saved by an appropriate use of machine-guided learning (in fields in which it makes sense), and allow those savings to be used to do the other kinds of teaching that are so important. This observation takes us back to the whole set of issues involving governance, decision-making, and resource allocation, writ large. These are issues that the academy really needs to think through because compartmentalized decision-making, the "every small tub on its own bottom" approach, is not going to get us where we need to go.

# APPENDIX TO THE PAPERBACK EDITION

# ACADEMIA ONLINE: MUSINGS (SOME UNCONVENTIONAL)[1]

## Stafford Little Lecture, Princeton University

## William G. Bowen

## October 14, 2013

IT IS HUMBLING TO BE part of a lecture series that dates from the time of President Cleveland and has included such luminaries as Albert Einstein and Gunnar Myrdal.

The topic I have chosen is "Academia Online: Musings (Some Unconventional)." So much has been said on the general subject of online learning that I run the risk of going over ground that is already familiar. To minimize that risk, I will begin by providing only the barest context. I will then discuss, in a "musing" mode with no claim of saying anything definitive, four ramifications of online learning that I regard as highly consequential: (1) "unbundling" of both faculty and institutional functions; (2) implications for the shape of the entire higher education sector; (3) impending changes in doctoral education; and (4) "equity" concerns that differ from those made famous by Myrdal, but that are no less challenging. (There is a fifth topic that is very important but that I pass over because of lack of time: namely, the implications of online technologies for "shared governance" and faculty roles in decision-making.) My focus will be on all of 4-year higher education in the U.S., not on Princeton. Princeton is—and will remain—an "outlier."

## Context

To attempt to estimate the current extent of online learning, or to enumerate its near-limitless forms, would be foolhardy. I spare all of us that exercise.[2] Suffice it to say that not a day passes without some new initiative or some new commentary on a phenomenon that is worldwide. Driving the proliferation of online offerings are three fundamental forces, which are likely to prove lasting.

- First, dramatic improvements in internet speed and availability, reductions in storage costs, and other technological advances have combined with changing mindsets to make possible a staggering variety of online formats that have captured the imagination of many teachers and scholars, especially those interested in reaching a wide audience.
- Second, this generation's students (the next generation's faculty members) embrace all things digital and expect to communicate in this way, whatever institution they attend.
- Third, there is a growing consensus in public discourse that current trends in both the cost of higher education and such outcomes as completion rates and time-to-degree are neither acceptable nor sustainable. There is no denying public impatience with tuition increases in higher education that have been driven in part by reductions in support (especially in state appropriations).[3] This impatience, coupled with a sense that "business as usual" will not suffice, has spurred a search for more cost-effective approaches than those we have known traditionally. Illustrative is President

Obama's continuing emphasis on the seriousness of this issue, his disappointment that higher education has not, on its own, done more to address the problem, and his renewed calls for action, complete with proposals for ways of addressing the problem.[4] There is, I fear, too much complacency in much of higher education—too much of a sense that if we just "hang in there," all will be well. Higher education needs to do its part—and then some—in adjusting to new realities.

Amidst all the argument over whether online learning is, in one form or another, a "good thing"—a solution to deep-seated problems or, in fact, a new problem of its own—there is general agreement that "the genie is out of the bottle." Online learning is, without question, here to stay. We can and should discuss—and with some urgency—how it can be improved, which audiences are best served by one approach or another, and what research teaches us about both learning outcomes and costs. There is, truth be told, far too little hard evidence available about what works and what cost savings, if any, can be anticipated. More rigorous research is desperately needed. Examples of flawed research abound.[5] In thinking about these issues, it is essential to compare "actuals" with "actuals" and to avoid the mistake of comparing an online offering with an idealized version of face-to-face teaching in some "golden age"—such as the opportunity Henry Cabot Lodge had to study medieval history with Henry Adams at Harvard.[6] We also know far too little about what actually works in face-to-face environments. New online initiatives should prod us to study rigorously the effectiveness of traditional modes of teaching as well as alternative approaches.[7]

The lack of much solid research notwithstanding, the world moves on. We can be confident that online learning, which is in its infancy, will improve. While there is still opportunity to affect outcomes, and to avoid unintended consequences that are undesirable, we should be giving serious thought to the broader implications of online technologies.

## Unbundling

Let us begin by considering the possible "unbundling" of both faculty and institutional roles in teaching. Over time, some faculty roles could change dramatically in an online world. When I was in charge of Economics 101 at Princeton in the halcyon days of yore, I was responsible for setting the syllabus of the course, crafting and giving lectures, working with others to plan the weekly sections that accompanied the lectures, leading one or two of the sections myself, responding to questions, counseling students (I recall asking one student who had great difficulty plotting points on a two-dimensional graph: "is this really the right subject for you?"), designing and supervising the grading of the tests used to evaluate student performance, and writing recommendations. Although I certainly had help, I thought of Economics 101 as "my course." Although in some ways independent, these various components of the course were all connected and bounded by geography—all of the participants in this educational experience were together in one place, Princeton.

Now, as a result of the digitization of information and its availability nearly everywhere on ubiquitous networks, new regimes beckon in at least some parts of higher education. One of my colleagues at ITHAKA (Richard Spies) has suggested that we imagine the debate at a less-privileged place than Princeton over who "owns" a course when

- the delivery platform comes from a MOOC producer (for-profit or not);

- much of the content comes from professors/lecturers at other universities (obtained through the MOOC producer, from the institutions employing those faculty members giving the lectures, from textbook providers, or even directly from the off-campus lecturer);
- automated online quizzes and advising tools come from yet another organization;
- teaching assistance and mentoring are provided by a shifting array of TAs, provided by the on-campus institution;
- and many kinds of support decisions are made by a central administration—the amount and kind of IT and other technical and administrative support provided, the number and qualifications of the TAs assigned to the course, legal support for agreements with third-party partners and perhaps even with on-campus faculty.

Moreover, these questions become even more complicated when we contemplate situations in which one of the original participants in creating this multi-dimensional course dies, retires, or moves to another institution. Or, suppose that one or another of the putative "owners" wishes to make the same course, or much of it, available to other campuses or to students with no campus affiliation—with or without compensation and with or without "credit" being offered. In prospect is a much more complicated world in which new thought will need to be given to who has (or should have) the authority to make decisions of various kinds concerning instructional methods.

Unbundling can of course occur not only at the level of the individual course but also across an institution's entire set of educational offerings—as more and more people in higher education recognize, often with fear and trembling and through clenched teeth. Unbundling at the institutional level could be highly consequential. The internet is the classic mechanism for unbundling, and we are all familiar with how lethal technology-driven unbundling has been in many sectors (note the loss of classified ads by newspapers and the success of Amazon in bypassing book stores). One trustee of a liberal arts college [Dan Currell] argues that:

> We haven't seen unbundled education at the college level yet...[in part] because colleges have kept education and evaluation tightly bundled together. The professor teaches *and* evaluates progress; the college offers courses *and* confers a degree....It won't necessarily stay this way. There is no reason why education and evaluation will necessarily stay bundled together, and one can already see movement in the direction of the two splitting apart.[8]

Currell is right; things need not stay as they are. It is easy to imagine, conceptually, colleges and universities unbundling a variety of functions (some kinds of advising, mentoring, evaluating, and even—heaven forbid—providing entertainment in the form of big-time football and basketball!). Of course, colleges and universities have for many years outsourced support functions such as food services and facilities management. Increasingly, in recent years, activities much closer to the academic heart of the institution have also been outsourced, such as access to scholarly journals—JSTOR. More fundamentally, we are already familiar with some degree of unbundling of course offerings, especially at the introductory level, via standard transfer mechanisms. More complex forms of transfer credit or credit for competency-based learning are clearly on the horizon.[9]

### The Shape of Things to Come: Seen "Through a Glass Darkly"

Now, let us contemplate the shape of things to come. The kinds of unbundling enabled by advances in technology and driven by worries about educational costs will have ramifications for the entire higher education sector that no one can foresee—hence, I think that those of us brave enough, or foolish enough, to speculate about such things need to be clear that we are viewing the future "through a glass darkly."

At one extreme, there is the proposition that the coming-of-age of online learning will have truly radical effects and will mean the demise—in whole or in large part—of face-to-face teaching and the residential model. As Peter Drucker asked back in 1989, "Will tomorrow's university be a 'knowledge centre' which transmits information rather than a place that students actually attend?"[10]

It is true that *some* forms of online learning can substitute for *some* forms of face-to-face instruction in *some* settings. This has happened already in parts of higher education, and especially for working adults in vocational fields.[11] Within the arts and sciences, colleagues and I demonstrated the cost-effectiveness of a well-designed Carnegie-Mellon statistics course, taught in a hybrid mode, at six mainstream public universities—we retained a limited amount of face-to-face interaction, and we used a random assignment methodology to avoid selection bias.[12] But the hybrid approach that we studied is a far cry from the model envisioned by the far more sweeping assertions about the impending demise of face-to-face teaching in its entirety. Such a development is not at all likely. Indeed, I believe it to be unthinkable. Our study used one sophisticated method of teaching a beginning course in a field, statistics, extremely well-suited to adaptive learning (there is, after all, one answer to the question of what is a *t*-test). It is far from obvious that the same pedagogy will work anything like as well in teaching subjects such as literature and international affairs. Face-to-face learning in many subjects and many settings will continue to persist for two very good reasons.

First, such teaching makes a great deal of educational sense, a priori, when we are trying to teach not only well-known concepts (the definition of a *t*-test), but also nuanced notions such as: how to frame questions in value-laden subjects, how to distinguish evidence from opinion, how to take account of different points of view, how to formulate one's own position on complex questions, how to express one's self verbally and in writing, how to engage with others as a member of an intellectual community, and even how to approach an understanding of "life lessons." Most fundamentally, we want to engender in students the excitement associated with encountering a new idea—an experience I first had, in full measure, as a graduate student at Princeton.[13]

A second reason for betting on the survival of good face-to-face teaching is that there will continue to be a demand for it. If application patterns are any guide (and, as a staunch believer in revealed preference, I think they are), a great many students and families will continue to pay dearly for the privilege of being part of a learning community that is about more than just acquisition of known concepts. Of course, the value proposition here includes much more than just the virtues of face-to-face teaching—it includes round-the-clock associations in settings conducive to give and take with a wonderfully diverse set of classmates. Such experiences can do wonders in the teaching of social skills as well as cognitive content, can provide invaluable opportunities to acquire leadership skills, and can lead to lifelong friendships. It would be a brave soul—and an uninformed soul, I would say—who would bet against this model perpetuating itself, even as we recognize that it will serve a small and highly privileged population which, in its demographics, is by no means a cross-section of all students.

Much more interesting than extreme models is the vast middle ground—where one can expect to find some online learning in a dizzying array of formats, in an innumerable variety of settings, and often used in conjunction with traditional forms of teaching.[14] Our system of higher education, if "system" is even the right word, is famously heterogeneous, and we are therefore blessed with literally hundreds (thousands?) of different educational models. New experiments are launched every day, and we are inundated with a surfeit of claims and counterclaims, most of them based on assertion rather than on evidence. It is my devout hope that we will indeed see "a hundred flowers bloom," and that we will avoid the stultifying effects of imitation and wrong-headed searches for a single right formula—that we will avoid forced standardization.

It would be splendid if the best of the burgeoning array of MOOCs could be harnessed to address at least some of the all-too-real challenges facing the large number of public colleges and universities that educate the vast majority of undergraduates in this country seeking BA degrees, as well as the army of community college students. But whether this is possible is an open question. We simply do not know. MOOCs were developed, after all, to reach vast numbers of individual students without reference to their institutional affiliation, if any, and without reference to existing educational infrastructures. They have demonstrated their capacity to engage large numbers of individuals all over the world (high drop-out rates notwithstanding), many of whom otherwise would have had no access to any form of higher education, and this is surely a splendid accomplishment. But engaging an individual student in a corner of India is very different from fitting within an institutional context and delivering good educational outcomes in a structured setting and in a cost-effective way. Modifying MOOCs to serve this large and highly consequential population entails very substantial technological *and* organizational challenges as we contemplate departures from the initial "one-size-fits-all" MOOC model. Right now, the ITHAKA organization is carrying out a study in collaboration with the University System of

Maryland to see what can be accomplished by using content and platforms created elsewhere to teach courses in a real-world institutional setting—recognizing that the hybrid courses we are testing are not really MOOCs, in that they are not "massive," not "open," and only partially "online."[15] As a former Princeton trustee, John Doar, said when leading the Nixon impeachment inquiry, "we will know more later." The jury is still out.

There are many other experiments underway. For example, the University of Texas at Austin has announced that, following almost a decade of research, two of its psychology professors will be offering what it calls "the world's first synchronous massive online course." The course will teach up to 10,000 students who must make themselves available at 6pm on Tuesdays and Thursdays and who will be charged a $550 registration fee. The class will be split into a number of smaller "pods" which will be monitored by former students who essentially work as online TAs. Students who finish the course will earn three transferrable credit hours. It will be exceedingly interesting to see the results of this undertaking—and to examine closely not only the educational outcomes, but also the all-in costs, which are hardly mentioned in a story about the UT initiative.[16]

Let me re-emphasize the importance of the cost blade of the online scissors. As I have said on other occasions, I am "more than bemused—actually I am dismayed"—by the lack of attention being paid, especially by faculty members, to the pressing need to control educational costs.[17] Unappealing as it may be to focus on costs (which, of course, can mean unwelcome changes in faculty staffing and in faculty roles), and satisfying as it may be to focus instead on the glories of teaching, in both old and new modes, it borders on the irresponsible to ignore the pressures to control costs—and the concomitant need to make the most intelligent, educationally-sensitive trade-offs that can be identified. To most observers, it is crystal clear that limits on available state funding have led to reduced appropriations to higher education which, in turn, have forced up tuition and often prevented fully offsetting increases in financial aid for needy students. It is simply wrong to suggest that cost savings made possible by technology have been the driving force in reducing state support; indeed, we have seen that efforts to control costs can lead to more sympathetic consideration of the need to sustain state funding.[18] Nor are reductions in state funding the only source of pressures to save money. Evidence available this fall (2013) reminds us that a number of institutions are also suffering from reduced enrollments.[19] Tuition-dependent private institutions seem especially vulnerable.

In seeking to contribute to the near-void of evidence as to what savings from the judicious use of online technologies might be achieved, ITHAKA, with support from the Spencer Foundation and the cooperation, once again, of the University System of Maryland, is embarking on a simulation of what educational costs might look like under a new regime, in which constraints on section sizes and the need to rely on existing plant and scheduling conventions are relaxed. The intention is to study the costs of a carefully-blended combination of online teaching and personalized instruction. It is entirely possible that scheduling innovations could themselves lead to improved completion rates and reduced time-to-degree, without anything like commensurate increases in costs. Such new approaches could also enable colleges and universities to educate larger numbers of both traditional and nontraditional students without anything like proportionate increases in faculty and other resources, a goal recognized by policymakers at both the federal and state levels to be highly important in meeting the needs of our increasingly knowledge-based economy. Online courses driven by sophisticated technology should also enable entirely new ways of studying how students learn, how to diagnose and fix common problems, and how to form new kinds of user communities. Technology should also enable us to find more cost-effective ways of discharging expensive support functions, such as advising.

To continue to muse about longer-term possibilities, I can envision a world in which more institutions adopt what I call a "portfolio" approach to curricular development. By this I mean that certain kinds of classes—and especially introductory courses in subjects in which, at least at this level, there is widespread agreement on "the right answer" to basic questions (beginning math is one example)—might be taught using online approaches, plus some admixture of advising, tutoring, and mentoring; resources saved in this way might be re-deployed, at least in part, to provide the personalized instruction in seminars and in directed study that can be so rewarding. Ideally, students would be assigned, or encouraged to choose, a mix of courses that would give them a well-calibrated exposure to various modes of teaching. Only in rare cases will instruction be exclusively online.

Over time, many institutions may want to import some online instruction, particularly in introductory courses in basic subjects such as beginning math and in advanced courses in a variety of fields that small colleges, for example, could not staff properly on their own. As I have argued in this book, there is much to be said for an intelligent division of labor, with those especially well-positioned to do so constructing sophisticated platforms with feedback loops, and with user campuses demonstrating at least modest capacity to customize offerings on the platform(s). We do not need a thousand versions of a basic/customizable platform; nor should we expect every campus to start from scratch in preparing its own online materials. Some wheels do not need to be re-invented.

Let me now acknowledge a pervasive problem in higher education that no one wants to talk about: the preoccupation of many in academia with what I hope will become antiquated notions of status. This is a difficult (nay, dreadful!) topic for me to discuss in this venue, at a university that is both very special to me and clearly at the top of any pecking order—but here I am, and so, as someone once said, Onward!

The more thoughtfully-integrated educational structure that I envision as a successor to the increasingly homogeneous university/college system now present depends on our taking advantage of economies of scale and contemplates different roles for different players, both institutions and individuals; it values complementarities. Some institutions and some individuals are surely better positioned to be leading "producers" of sophisticated platforms and other content than are others. I also suspect that some institutions and individuals are better positioned than others (perhaps more temperamentally suited) to be extremely skillful consumers of content that originates mostly, if not entirely, elsewhere.

To be sure, different kinds of talent exist almost everywhere, and we should be careful not to exclude anyone from creative tasks for arbitrary reasons linked to wrong-headed notions of status. In fact, I suspect that market mechanisms will help achieve a sorting of people, institutions, and functions—which is certainly desirable from a system-wide perspective. At the same time, refusing to recognize the existence of institutional differences would be foolish. Some places are fortunate to have an unusually powerful combination of intellectual and financial resources—a combination that is sometimes tied to scale and even to institutional culture. If the institutions especially well-positioned to make significant contributions to the development of course content and delivery mechanisms do so effectively, all of higher education will benefit. But this is certainly not to say that institutions especially well-suited to be "producers" (Princeton may well be among them) should be excused from paying attention to the system-wide need to control cost increases. Ideally, they would be outstanding examples of the ability to achieve excellent educational outcomes at manageable cost.

In thinking about status issues, we need to recognize that human nature is what it is—we are not, as President Eisgruber said so eloquently in his inaugural address, "angels." Still, I think we should do our best to resist "above and below the salt" thinking. At the end of some future day, the real kudos may go to the highly-creative institutional *assemblers* of intellectual content and local teaching resources. There should be a real pay-off to institutions that are especially skillful in harvesting content provided by others and then adding educationally-rich value of their own, including mentoring.

A closely related point is that, as Hanna Holborn Gray has suggested, major universities, and especially the multiversities that Clark Kerr made famous, should ask hard questions about the wide range of activities that many of them now undertake—in part in response to the initiatives of others. No one wants to be left behind, seemingly unable to compete for the n'th full-paying student. The rise of "consumerism" is a reality and can easily lead to what the historian Laurence R. Veysey once called "blind imitation"—to the search by essentially all universities for a "complete" course of study and the provision of innumerable student services. In her book aptly titled *Searching for Utopia,* President Gray offers this provocative insight:

> It seems clear that universities need to confront some painful realities and become more deliberately selective in what they choose to do. Universities are overstretched in their range of programs, overbuilt in physical facilities, and overburdened by an excess of ambitions, expectations, and demands. The competition among

them has led to greater homogeneity rather than constructive diversity of institutional profiles and of distinctive individual excellence. We would be better off if it were possible....to build on each institution's comparative strengths...Greater differentiation among institutions might encourage each to focus on its own particular mix of academic priorities...[20]

She ends her commentary by urging a rebalancing of the elements of what she calls "the stripped down university."[21]

It is by no means obvious how this country's present educational system can move in the direction which President Gray advocates, since both current structures and assumptions about unending growth are deeply ingrained. But, well-crafted incentives at the state level might make a difference in the public sector. Additional research on the costs of various programs, and their relation to student learning, might make a difference across the board.

## Doctoral Education: Impending Changes?

There is one super-sensitive set of activities that I feel an obligation to at least allude to, even as I recognize the pain and suffering sure to afflict anyone who even mentions this subject, never mind someone with my long ties to a prestigious university such as Princeton. I refer to the scale of doctoral education in this country, seen now in relation to ongoing trends in faculty deployment that are, in part, directly related to the combination of cost pressures and the spread of online technologies.

The current sorry state of the job market for new doctorates, trained in the traditional way, is hardly a secret.[22] There has been, without doubt, a pronounced decrease in the demand by colleges and universities for new recipients of PhDs. The intense cost pressures felt by many colleges and universities have led to both a felt need to curb faculty payrolls and an increased desire for staffing flexibility. The growth of online programs has had its own effects, by reducing both the current and prospective need for "regular" faculty trained as teacher/scholars, and for individuals prepared to teach all aspects of their "own courses" in the traditional way.[23] The potential unbundling of faculty roles suggests that we may be moving toward a situation in which higher education in general needs relatively fewer "all purpose" teacher-scholars, and a larger number of individuals prepared to fill more specialized roles at various kinds of institutions.

One consequence of the incipient stages of these trends evident already is the substitution of adjuncts (part-time faculty) for regular faculty. Those of us inclined to focus our attention on the most privileged institutions (such as members of this audience) may be surprised by the magnitude of what has transpired already. David Figlio and his colleagues at Northwestern have summarized data documenting the dramatic decline in the share of all faculty (excluding graduate students) in the tenure system: the fraction declined from 57 percent in 1975 to 30 percent in 2009, and it is still falling. Figlio et al also report the results of a most interesting study at their own university which suggests that non-tenure-line faculty teaching introductory courses contributed more than regular faculty to lasting student learning.[24] These learning outcomes, based on work in introductory courses, are presumably very different from the learning that occurs through directed study and seminars, formats in which I would think regular faculty enjoy a real advantage. In any case, many institutions have concluded that adjuncts both cost less than regular faculty and provide more staffing flexibility.

Another factor to consider is the prospective reduction in the need for Teaching Assistants (TAs) that is likely to result from greater use of adaptive learning technologies (machine-guided learning) in many introductory courses. It is, of course, the current need for a large number of TAs that justifies (and pays for) the scale of many doctoral programs.[25]

These developments come on top of "pre-existing conditions" in doctoral education that would be serious enough without these added stresses. Robert M. Berdahl, when he was president of the Association of American Universities (AAU), once courageously asked "How many research universities does the nation require?" He added: "I do not know how many we should have. But it is a serious question, worthy of consideration."[26] Nor are these new concerns. In the early 1990s, Neil Rudenstine and I assembled data documenting the remarkable increase in the number and growth of doctoral programs, especially those less highly ranked, during the expansionist years between 1958 and 1972. During the subsequent "lean years," the relative share of doctorates awarded by these newer and lower-ranked programs increased dramatically.[27]

As Berdahl's failed attempt to get people to focus on this question illustrates all too clearly, it is extremely difficult to modify, never mind eliminate, programs that grew up in different times. And it is of course easy to understand why institutions that are the home of what one has to acknowledge are "middling" doctoral programs want to hold on to them. Someone once said that such programs are the "soft underbelly" of American higher education. This is, in my view, the right time to face up to the growing imbalance between supply and demand in doctoral education. We need to own up to reality. We need to recognize that, as President Hennessy of Stanford said bluntly in a discussion session following one of my Tanner Lectures in 2012, we are producing too many PhDs; we are going to have to accept the fact that in the future there will be fewer "regular" faculty positions than there are today.[28]

Market pressures may begin to compel changes. One might expect some prospective graduate students to shy away from doctoral programs because of evident job-market concerns—but recent data showing an unexpected boost in doctoral enrollment in the humanities offer a puzzling piece of evidence to the contrary.[29] It is true that, as one person said, "we live in a free country," and if people are informed of job prospects, they should be allowed "to pursue their dreams."[30] But such pursuits are far from cost free to the society at large.

In the public sector, in particular, both individual institutions and legislators may be more and more reluctant to support the expensive infrastructure that doctoral education requires. It is hard to know if the decision of the University of Florida to end its doctoral program in economics is any kind of harbinger.[31] Whatever the preferences of individual institutions, legislators may be reluctant to support positions at non-research universities for traditionally-trained faculty—especially in settings in which it is far from obvious that research capacities are going to be required of all those engaged in an unbundled set of teaching responsibilities. The purely economic consequences of moving from one staffing model to another could be considerable; what is sometimes called "departmental research" (building into the calculation of teaching loads an assumption that all faculty must be given some time for traditional research, aimed at publication) is very expensive. As Richard Spies puts it: "research wannabes are a luxury—or maybe an inefficiency—that we will find it hard to pay for in the future."[32]

A danger, of course, is that such pressures will be excessive and will threaten support for the high quality research, and the high quality doctoral training, that will continue to be of critical importance. The key, as always, is to find a magical balance: to support "enough" but not "too much." But I am definitely in the camp of those who believe that we are out of balance today in the "too much" direction" and need to realign our overall "system" of graduate education so that it will work more effectively in a changed (and changing) environment.

A related question of major consequence is whether renewed thought should be given to "teaching doctorates"—or at least to paying increasing attention to questions such as how to teach graduate students the skills needed to impart the kinds of education that simply cannot be provided online. I think, along with Michael McPherson, that there is a real opportunity here for academia writ large to address positively, and not just negatively, the implications of the spread of online learning. [33] Another colleague, Eugene Tobin, who has wide experience with liberal arts colleges, adds: "In an ironic way, the special human dimensions of teaching…, including understanding how to 'flip' the classroom with more than the use of technology, may be one of every future faculty member's most needed skills." [34] Our studies at ITHAKA suggest that faculty are very open, even eager, to move in this direction. Whether doctoral programs will have the interest, or the capacity, to respond to such ideas is an open question—and a very important one.

## Equity Issues

I end these musings by calling attention to what I regard as one of the most important issues to ponder as we look ahead: implications of the spread of online learning for "equity." Will the development of various forms of online learning help level the playing field or exacerbate the already large divide between educational haves and have-nots? I ask this question even as I agree with those who argue that this divide is driven largely by factors such as income inequality which are not primarily the responsibility of higher education—culprits abound! [35] Still, I want to retain my focus on online learning. One of the founders of Coursera, Daphne Koller, has been eloquent in arguing that a major contribution of MOOCs is the opening of educational opportunity to students all over the world, regardless of their circumstances.[36] It would be ironic indeed if the whole gamut of online offerings were to have the perverse effect in the U.S. of increasing, rather than reducing, disparities in educational outcomes. This is, regrettably, entirely possible.

Let's start with Princeton. This university is making a commendable effort to see if there are ways to take advantage of technology to improve what is already an outstanding educational program. In my view, it is highly likely that the strongest liberal arts colleges, as well as the leading universities, will only get better as a result of opportunities created by advances in technology. The "haves" are not at risk. And because of generous financial aid policies, these privileged institutions will continue to offer exceptional educational opportunities not only to the well-qualified children of affluent families (who are present in large numbers in their applicant pools), but also to top students from lower income families. But the absolute number of such fortunate students from modest backgrounds will be small. As Joseph Stiglitz has put it, the problem is not that "social mobility is impossible, but that the upwardly mobile American is becoming a statistical rarity."[37] Princeton will, I am confident, continue to make the direct contributions that it can to educating a diverse student body of high talent. And I hope that it will also seek ways, many of them less direct and involving its research arm and its leadership capacities, to contribute to the broader national challenge that is before us.

But what does online learning portend for less privileged educational institutions? What about the offerings available to students attending the mid-level public institutions and the community colleges that educate such a high proportion of our undergraduates? As public support for higher education diminishes, students at these institutions are increasingly the "have nots." Will they too benefit, alongside undergraduates at the Princetons and Haverfords, from the spread of online technologies? That is certainly the hope. However, comments by some governors, feeding on the over-hyped promise of truly minimalist online offerings, suggest that inexpensive online programs, lacking in feedback loops and any real human component, could tempt states to try to meet their educational obligations "on the cheap." Such a development, if it happens, could widen substantially the existing gap between the haves and the have-nots. The less-affluent, less-well-prepared students are poor candidates for cookie-cutter online offerings. A widely discussed study by Columbia's Teacher's College found compelling evidence that online offerings were not equally effective with all kinds of students.[38]

Jennifer Morton, an Assistant Professor at CUNY, has written eloquently about the needs of her students, many of whom are first-generation college-goers and/or recent immigrants from low income families, for the social skills that can be helped greatly by inspired face-to-face teaching. How to make eye contact, to speak up before strangers, and to defend a position in an unfamiliar setting—these are precisely the skills that she believes her students have to be helped to acquire. Children of middle-class families often learn to navigate social relationships at home, but that is often not an option for Professor Morton's students. The danger, she suggests, is that the substitution of low-level online instruction for face-to-face teaching may simply aggravate problems that are already evident in many lecture-only settings, or in any setting in which faculty do not seek to impart the kinds of social skills that are so important for success in job searches and, for that matter, in life.[39] As she recognizes, much face-to-face teaching also fails abysmally in this area—but that is hardly an argument for mindlessly substituting an educational option that is equally poorly suited to meeting real needs.

I am driven back to my advocacy of a portfolio approach to curricular development: not every course needs to have the features Professor Morton champions, and it is probably unrealistic, for financial and other reasons, to have that as our goal. Also, I recognize that the concern I have expressed about the bad qualities of some forms of online learning may lead some to advocate staying out of the online game altogether. But that is hardly an answer. What is needed is the ability, and the willingness, to develop effective online pedagogies that can then be employed, in properly limited ways, in different settings, and with different student populations. My cautionary musings are meant only to heighten our awareness of a serious danger if we approach all forms of online learning with a one-size-fits-all mentality, and treat them as cure-alls, appropriate in every context.

We must believe in education as an engine of social mobility—and act on that belief. The Pledge of Allegiance refers, after all, to "one nation ... indivisible." We need to take great care that in our search for cost-effective ways of educating we not lose sight of the need to teach *all* students in cost-effective ways appropriate to their needs. It would be a tragedy, and nothing less than that, if new approaches to teaching widened the divide between the haves and the have-nots in our society.[40]

## Notes to the Appendix to the Paperback Edition

1. I wish to thank Lawrence S. Bacow, Kevin M. Guthrie, Deanna Marcum, Michael S. McPherson, Christine Mulhern, Richard Spies, Eugene M. Tobin, Sarah E. Turner, and Derek Wu for many helpful comments on earlier drafts of this talk. I also wish to thank Johanna Brownell for her invaluable help with the preparation of a final version.

2. My former colleague, Kelly Lack, and I attempt to provide a kind of "reader's guide" to the online learning landscape, pp. 72–77.

3. For an unusually explicit statement of a direct link between state funding decisions and tuition increases, see: Brendan Bures, "Tuition

increase imminent for FSU; Barron obligated to hike costs against wishes," *FSU News*, August 25, 2013.

4. See Michael D. Shear, "Obama to Offer Plans to Ease Burden of Paying for College," *New York Times,* August 21, 2013, online edition. Also see "FACT SHEET on the President's Plan to Make College More Affordable: A Better Bargain for the Middle Class," Office of the Press Secretary, The White House, August 22, 2013, and Kelly E. Field, "Obama's Lofty Goals on College Costs Face Long Odds," *Chronicle of Higher Education*, August 28, 2013.

5. In September 2013, there was a report on a project at San Jose State involving a "test" of the effectiveness of a Udacity offering, and I put "test" in quotes precisely because of the problems with this "research." Particularly striking is the obvious power of selection effects (allowing students with different backgrounds and predilections to choose the teaching format that they prefer). As many of those who have commented on this project recognize, we just have to do much better than this "test" if we are to get anywhere in studying both learning outcomes for various groups of students and the costs of various kinds of "treatments." See Carl Straumsheim, "The Full Report on Udacity Experiment," *Inside Higher Ed*, September 12, 2013. See also the earlier article by the same author, "San Jose State U posts improved online course results, but Udacity partnership remains on pause," *Inside Higher Ed* August 28, 2013. Particularly striking are the methodological problems, combined with the disappointing results for Udacity's entry-level math offering—presumably "favorable" selection effects notwithstanding. Various individuals in the California system are reported to be (properly) skeptical about the allegedly positive results cited in earlier reports.

6. See Hunter Rawling's remarks at the installation of President Eisgruber at Princeton University, September 22, 2013, in which he quotes Henry Cabot Lodge with respect to a course he had taken at Harvard:

> "In all my four years, I never really studied anything, never had my mind roused to any exertion or to anything resembling active thought until in my senior year I stumbled into the course in medieval history given by Henry Adams, who had then just come to Harvard.... [Adams] had the power not only of exciting interest, but he awakened opposition to his own views, and this is one great secret of success in teaching...I worked hard in that course because it gave me pleasure. I took the highest marks, for which I cared, as I found, singularly little, because marks were not my object, and for the first time I got a glimpse of what education might be and really learned something.... Yet it was not what I learned but the fact that I learned something, that I discovered that it was the keenest of pleasures to use one's mind, a new sensation, and one which made Mr. Adams's course in the history of

the Middle Ages so memorable to me." [Gary Wills, *Henry Adams and the Making of America*, New York, NY 2005, p. 89.]

My thoughts on how to improve online learning (in different contexts and for different pedagogies), and how we should be thinking about studies of the effectiveness of learning outcomes and potential cost savings, are throughout, especially pp. 46–61.

7. See my remarks at the upcoming Inauguration of Daniel Weiss as President of Haverford, October 26, 2013.

8. See Dan Currell, "In tempestuous times, colleges must decide what they're for (essay)," *Inside Higher Ed*, June 28, 2013. Currell is a trustee of Gustavus Adolphus College, and executive director with the Legal, Risk and Compliance Practice at the Corporate Executive Board. See Scott Jaschik, "Obama's Ratings for Higher Ed," *Inside Higher Ed*, August 22, 2013: "The White House also said President Obama is 'challenging' colleges to 'adopt one or more' of practices he called 'promising' to 'offer break-throughs on cost, quality or both.' Among them: competency-based learning that moves away from seat time, course redesign (including massive open online courses), the use of technology for student services, and more efforts to recognize prior learning."

9. See Paul Fain, "Competency-based Transcripts," *Inside Higher Ed*, August 9, 2013. See also Jeffrey J. Selingo, "The New Nonlinear Path through College," *Chronicle of Higher Education*, September 30, 2013, and Scott Carlson, "Competency-based Education Goes Mainstream in Wisconsin," *Chronicle of Higher Education*, October 1, 2013.

10. See Peter F. Drucker, *The New Realities*, Elsevier, Great Britain, 1989, p. 249

11. See Paul Fain, "Experimental College's First Graduate," *Inside Higher Ed*, August 16, 2013.

12. See William G. Bowen, Matthew M. Chingos, Kelly A. Lack, and Thomas I. Nygren, "Interactive Learning Online at Public Universities: Evidence from Randomized Trials," May 22, 2012, available on the ITHAKA website at www.sr.ithaka.org.

13. The eyes of one of my great teachers, Jacob Viner, sparkled when he demonstrated the intense pleasure of engagement with a new way of thinking. He taught me, and many others, that learning is great fun—a lesson that has had a lifelong impact on me. But I recognize, as one of my colleagues has pointed out to me, that this kind of experience is all too rare.

14. See, for example, the account of the growth of various kinds of online courses at Iowa State University: "Enrollment, student demand fuels growth for online courses at ISU," posted Aug. 26, 2013, Iowa State University News Service, http://www.news.iastate.edu/news/2013/08/26/online-courses.

15. See "Informing Innovation in Higher Education: Evidence from Implementing the Latest Online Learning Technologies in a Public

University System," Ithaka S + R, November 8, 2012. http://www.sr.ithaka. org/research-publications/informing-innovation-higher-education-evidence-implementing-latest-online. Interim report forthcoming. This work at Maryland reminds me powerfully of the value of the enthusiasm and creativity of individual faculty members—which need to be treasured, not just tolerated, and certainly not repressed. But such creativity does need to be channeled.

16. See Carl Straumsheim, "UT Psychology Professors Prepare 'World's First' Synchronous Massive Online Course," *Inside Higher Ed*, August 27, 2013. The professors report that the research that led up to this offering demonstrated that their adaptive learning approach produced both better overall grades and a reduction in the achievement gap between upper, middle, and lower-income students. See Also Ry Rivard, "Georgia Tech and Udacity Roll Out Massive New Low-cost Degree Program," *Inside Higher Ed*, May 14, 2013. Georgia Tech plans to offer a Master's program for a fraction of the cost (less than $7000/year versus the standard program cost of $40,000 per year) to 10,000 students online.

17. See William G. Bowen, *Higher Education in the Digital Age*, Princeton University Press, 2013, and William G. Bowen, "The Potential for Online Learning: Promises and Pitfalls," *EDUCAUSE Review,* vol. 48, no. 5 (September/October 2013).

18. One telling example of the direction of causation is provided by experience in the state of Maryland, where the university system reached a "compact" of sorts with the state. As the Chancellor, William ("Brit") Kirwan explains [personal correspondence, September 7, 2013]: "In return for a systematic and sustained effort at cost containment, the state agreed to protect our budget, at least in relative terms and in effect 'buy down' tuition increases with general funds." Kirwan is scathing in his dismissal of the proposition that institutions should avoid seeking cost-effective reductions in educational costs. This argument, in Kirwan's words, "epitomizes why higher education is in such trouble." He goes on to say: "Few outside higher education could understand an argument that says, 'if an institution might produce better results with lower costs, then you should abandon the initiative.'" There is also abundant evidence from other states that reductions in state support have occurred in the absence of cost-saving innovations.

19. As of last May, 59 percent of private bachelor's institutions and 77 percent of public master's or bachelor's institutions had failed to meet enrollment targets. See Scott Jaschik, "Feeling the Heat: The 2013 Survey of College and University Admissions Directors," *Inside Higher Ed*, September 18, 2013, and Eric Hoover and Beckie Supiano, "In Admissions, Old Playbook is Being Revised," *Chronicle of Higher Education*, September 16, 2013.

20. See Hanna Gray, *Searching for Utopia*, University of California Press, 2013, p. 94. After citing Veysey, President Gray gives a sobering account of recent trends ( pp. 78ff).

21. Gray, *Searching for Utopia*, p. 96.

22. See David Mihalyfy, "Regilding the Ivory Tower," *Inside Higher Ed*, June 18, 2013.

23. See William G. Bowen, Matthew M. Chingos, Kelly A. Lack, and Thomas I. Nygren, "Interactive Learning Online at Public Universities: Evidence from Randomized Trials," May 22, 2012, for very crude estimates of the potential effects of one online course on the mix of faculty needed. This crude simulation is but the tip of the proverbial iceberg, and it will be important to look closely at the results of the cost simulations the ITHAKA team is going to prepare for much more refined estimates of possible longer-term effects.

24. See David N. Figlio, Morton O. Schapiro, and Kevin B. Soter, "Are Tenure Track Professors Better Teachers?" NBER Working Paper, 19406, September 2013. The authors also cite a number of other studies of teaching effectiveness, measured in different ways, of various categories of faculty/teachers.

25. My colleague, Lawrence S. Bacow, has emphasized repeatedly the importance of TAs in driving decisions of all kinds concerning doctoral programs. Thus, he has observed: "As online learning becomes more prevalent, I think it is likely that the demand for TAs and the allocation of them across disciplines is likely to shift. Assuming that deans and provosts respond accordingly, some departments are likely to see reductions in the number of TAs they are allotted and others may see increases.... I think this has big consequences for the size of graduate programs in the affected departments. Moreover, if a department cannot support the same number of graduate students through TAships, over time the size of the department may shrink (or at least it should in my mind); of course, some may also increase. My point is that online education, depending upon how it ultimately gets implemented, could have very large consequences for the size of various graduate programs." (Personal correspondence, August 12, 2013).

26. See Robert M. Berdahl, "Reassessing the Value of Research Universities," *Chronicle of Higher Education*, July 13, 2009, online edition.

27. See William G. Bowen and Neil L. Rudenstine, *In Pursuit of the PhD*, Princeton University Press, 1992, Chapter 4. Roughly 30 years earlier, in 1960, Bernard Berelson used colorful language to describe the forces that stimulate the growth of new doctoral programs, noting: "the colonization of the underdeveloped institutions by ambitious products of the developed ones who then work to make the colony a competitor of the mother university; the need to have graduate students as research and teaching assistants, partly in order to get and hold senior staff; the vanity, pride, and legitimate aspirations of the institutions." Bernard Berelson, *Graduate Education in the United States*, McGraw-Hill, NY, 1960, p. 35.

28. See n. 32. P. 33.

29. Data released by the Council of Graduate Schools this September [2013] are summarized by Scott Jaschik, "Humanities Doctoral Programs

Show Unexpected Boost in New Students," *Inside Higher Education*, September 12, 2013.

30. See quote attributed to Debra Stewart in *Inside Higher Ed*, September 12, 2013

31. See Stacey Patton, "Once Flourishing Economics PhD Program Prepares to Die," *Chronicle of Higher Education*, September 10, 2013, online edition. It should be noted that prospects for graduates of PhD programs in economics are better than prospects for doctorate recipients in many other fields. But the costs to institutions of offering such programs are still far from negligible, as this story illustrates. The fact that this program is offered within a business school rather than within an arts and sciences program may be relevant in assessing the likelihood that other institutions will make similar decisions.

32. Personal correspondence, September 2, 2013.

33. Here is the way that Michael S. McPherson, president of the Spencer Foundation and a wise observer of this scene, puts it: "To have a solid academic career, at least outside the top research universities, a PhD in most fields will either need to be a really outstanding scholar/researcher or will have to be able to teach effectively in ways that computers can't easily match. We don't know for sure what those hard-to-match qualities are, but they certainly aren't going to be straightforward content delivery. This suggests to me that it may become necessary for graduate schools to take more seriously than they have the problem of preparing their students to teach well in those ways that require human qualities that we don't know how to match online. This is a very hard problem because what teaching well in college means, if we mean by good teaching more than giving high quality lectures, is not well understood." [Personal correspondence, August 9, 2013.]

34. Personal correspondence, August 9, 2013.

35. See Catherine B. Hill, "Higher Education's Biggest Challenge is Income Inequality," *The Washington Post*, September 6, 2013.

36. See Daphne Koller, "How Online Education Can Create a 'Global 'Classroom,'" CNN International, June 21, 2013. http://edition.cnn.com/2013/06/21/business/opinion-koller-education-petersburg-forum/index.html

37. See Joseph E. Stiglitz, "Equal Opportunity, our National Myth," *New York Times*, February 16, 2013.

38. See Shanna Smith Jaggars and Thomas Bailey, "Effectiveness of Fully Online Courses for College Students: Response to a Department of Education Meta-Analysis," Community College Research Center, Teacher's College Columbia University (July 2010). It should have surprised no one to learn that students from modest backgrounds with less well thought out educational aspirations were much more likely than other students to drop out of online courses. Commenting on early experience with the much-touted Udacity/San Jose State effort to use online teaching, Lillian Taiz,

president of the California Faculty Association, noted that pass rates were especially low in San Jose State's remedial math course. See Carl Straumsheim, "San Jose State U, posts improved online course results, but Udacity partnership remains on pause," *Inside Higher Ed*, August 28, 2013.

39. Jennifer Morton, "Unequal Classrooms: What Online Education Cannot Teach," *Chronicle of Higher Education*, August 29, 2013. My colleagues at ITHAKA believe that over time communities made possible by technology will create at least partial substitutes for the class-room discussions that many of us remember with such pleasure.

40. See Elizabeth Reddem. "Higher Education in 2020," *Inside Higher Ed*, September 26, 2013, for a dire warning that government pressures to drive down the costs of degrees could lead, in an unbundled online environment, to a situation in which "The cultural divide between the elite and the rest will widen in the US and the UK."

# INDEX

Page numbers for entries occurring in figures are followed by an *f* and those for entries in notes, by an *n*.

Baum, Sandy, 4, 22, 26, 28n6, 33n33, 36n45, 36nn47–48, 37n52, 38nn56–57, 41n75
Baumol, William J., 3, 4, 25, 27n2, 27n4, 41n72, 47–48, 79n12, 124, 135, 158–59
Belkin, Douglas, 30n17
Berdahl, Robert M., 15, 33n30
Berkner, Lutz, 38–39n62
Bezos, Jeff, 69–70, 94n71, 142
Bienen, Henry S., 80n13
Bill & Melinda Gates Foundation, 24, 53, 153
blended learning. *See* hybrid-format courses
Bok, Derek, 8, 23, 29n12, 39nn65–66, 47, 91n58
*Boston* magazine, 132, 133f
Bound, John, 33n33
Bowen, Howard, 31n21
Bowen, William G., 3, 4, 8, 15, 23, 27nn1–2, 27nn4–5, 29n12, 31n18, 32n25, 33n27, 33n29, 34nn35–36, 34nn39–40, 38n61, 39nn65–67, 77–78nn1–3, 78n7, 80n15, 81–82nn18–19, 82nn22–23, 83n28, 90n56, 92n66, 129–30
Bowen's Law, 2. *See also* cost disease
Brooks, David, 142
Brown, Gordon, 156
Brown, Tina, 130

California: community colleges in, 34n35, 151–52; enrollment caps in, 40n70; higher education funding in, 25
Cambridge University, 92n64
Carey, Kevin, 84–85n33
Carnegie Commission on the Future of Higher Education, 2
Carnegie Mellon University (CMU), 58, 64. *See also* ITHAKA study of hybrid-format statistics course; Open Learning Initiative
Carroll, C. Dennis, 38–39n62
Chakrabarti, Rajashri, 36n46
Chance, Beth, 81n16
cheating, 84–85n33, 99
Chingos, Matthew M., 22, 32n25, 34nn35–36, 34nn39–40, 38n58, 38n61, 39n67, 40n70, 80n15

Christensen, Clayton, 136
City University of New York (CUNY), 17, 34n38, 48
Clark, M. H., 83–84n29
Class2Go platform, 59, 86–87n40
Clobridge, Abby, 78–79n10
Clotfelter, Charles T., 11, 31n20
CMU. *See* Carnegie Mellon University
cognitive science, 53, 58, 81–82n19, 94–95n73
cognitive tutors, 48, 73, 76, 80n14
Cohen, Jennifer, 38n62
Cohodes, Sarah, 34–35n40
collaboration: among universities, 103–5, 127; challenges of, 127; international, 105–6
College Board, 19, 37n52
College of St. Scholastica, 83n24
Columbia University, 31–32n23, 134
communications technology, 8, 146
communities, 100–101, 102, 103
community colleges: capacities of, 34n35, 151–52; hybrid-format courses at, 53, 79n11, 86n40, 152; students of, 131
completion rates: cost reductions and, 120, 160–61; crisis of, 24, 119; declines in, 152; economic impact of, 119; efforts to raise, 24; impact of online learning, 52, 54, 153; of low-income students, 24, 40n70; at selective institutions, 17–18, 35n42; by type of institution, 119
computer science classes, 53, 61, 74, 85n35, 88–89n47, 152
Cook, Thomas D., 83n29
Cornell University, 10, 94n72, 95n77, 105
cost disease, 3–4, 25, 27n5, 70, 135–36
costs of higher education: compared to other industries, 109–10; competitive pressures and, 11–15, 32n24; completion rates and, 120, 160–61; controlling, 62, 89–90n52; data sources on, 28–29n6; factors in rise of, 9–18, 29–30n14, 30n17, 31n20; fixed, 11; impact of online learning, 70, 84–85n33, 136, 149, 151; inefficiencies and, 9–11; infrastructure, 52; instructional methods and, 64; measurement of, 33n34; net cost of attendance, 112;

Martin, Andrew, 38n55
Massachusetts Institute of Technology (MIT): collaboration with Harvard, 103–4; cost increases at, 11–12; MITx, 40–41n70, 53, 61, 86–87n40; Open-CourseWare, 60; presidents of, 88n45, 89n49; Singapore campus, 105. *See also* edX
massive open online courses (MOOCs): advantages of, 153–54; anti-cheating measures in, 84–85n33, 99; business models of, 60, 61, 87–88n44, 140; costs of, 53, 59–60; customization options, 59–60; description of, 73–74, 78–79n10; evaluations of, 47, 52–53, 55, 61, 79n11, 87n42, 140; fees for, 60, 87–88n44, 89n49; media coverage of, 59, 70; non-credit-bearing, 74, 78–79n10, 84n32; organizations offering, 74; potential impact of, 54–55, 60–61, 84–85n33, 93–94n69; potential uses of, 54–55, 86–87n40, 89–90n52, 153–54; productivity improvements from, 55; social networking aspects of, 85–86n36, 92–93n66; student characteristics, 61, 88–89n47, 154; time spent by students, 84n32; transfer credits for, 55, 84–85n33, 86n40, 87n42, 89–90n52, 153. *See also* Coursera; edX
Mazur, Eric, 150
McAdory, Alice, 78n4
McKinsey & Company, 30n16
McPherson, Michael S., 4, 22, 26, 28n6, 32n25, 33n33, 34nn35–36, 34nn39–40, 36n45, 38nn56–57, 38n61, 39n67, 41n75, 48–49
Means, Barbara, meta-analysis of, 78n9
Medicaid, 114–15
medical schools, 93n67, 113
Medina, Jonathan, 41n74
Mellon Foundation, 15, 80n13
mental health services, 116
Middaugh, Michael F., 28n6
Miller, Ben, 91n58, 95n74
mismatch problem, 17–18, 23, 34–35nn40–42
MIT. *See* Massachusetts Institute of Technology

Mitchell, Josh, 38n54
MITx, 40–41n70, 53, 61, 86–87n40
MOOCs. *See* massive open online courses
Moody's, 24
Mossberg, Walt, 88n46

NACUBO. *See* National Association of College and University Business Officers
National Academy of Sciences, 6
National Association of College and University Business Officers (NACUBO), 31–32n23
National Center for Academic Transformation (NCAT), 72, 82n21, 91n58
National Center for Education Statistics (NCES), 22–23, 28n6, 38–39n62
National Collegiate Athletics Association (NCAA), 13
National Survey of Student Engagement (NSSE), 37n51, 38n61
Navarro, Peter, 78n2
NCAA. *See* National Collegiate Athletics Association
NCAT. *See* National Center for Academic Transformation
NCES. *See* National Center for Education Statistics
*New England Journal of Medicine* (*NEJM*), 6–7, 54
Newfield, Christopher, 29n7
*Newsweek*, 130, 131f
New York City public schools, 103
*New York Times*, 21–22, 38n56, 114
New York University (NYU), 105
Ng, Andrew, 84nn32–33, 87–88n44
Noer, Michael, 82n20
NSSE. *See* National Survey of Student Engagement
Nygren, Thomas I., 80n15
NYU. *See* New York University

Obama, Barack, 24, 39–40n68, 41n71
OCW. *See* OpenCourseWare
OLI. *See* Open Learning Initiative
Olin College, 104
One Day University, 138
online learning: adaptive learning, 44, 58, 160; advantages of, 147; appeal of,

productivity improvements (*continued*)
  in numerator or denominator of ratio,
  7–8, 9, 50–51, 65, 148, 149; from
  online learning, 52, 54–55, 149–53,
  160–61; output increases, 7–8, 9; public demand for, 26; time-to-degree, 52,
  54, 160–61
provocation, 140–42, 157–58
public universities: completion rates of,
  119; cost trends at, 113–14; enrollment caps in, 25, 36n44, 40n70; federal support of, 19, 63; financial aid at,
  19, 21; funding cuts for, 5, 19, 25,
  36n44, 41n71, 113, 114–15, 152; performance goals for, 26, 41n76; public
  support of, 25, 63; resource allocation
  in, 161; time-to-degree increases at,
  16–17; tuition at, 5, 19, 20f, 21, 25,
  36n46, 113–14

rankings, 13, 89n51, 125, 126
Reardon, Sean F., 40n70
Reed, Charlie, 41n71
reflection sessions, 103
Reif, L. Rafael, 88n45, 89n49
research: costs of, 113, 116, 117–18;
  funding of, 113, 118; methodologies
  of, 48, 53–54, 81n18, 83–84nn28–30;
  technology use in, 8–9
research universities, 15, 117–18
residential education: advantages of,
  67–68, 98–101, 106–7; amenities of,
  13, 32n24, 102, 116, 124, 130–31; disadvantages of, 99; ideals, 100–101;
  improving, 101–6; international collaboration, 105–6; net cost of attendance, 112; retaining best features of,
  67–70, 99–100, 161; room and board
  costs in, 111, 112; technology use in,
  73
returns to education, 20–21, 37nn51–52,
  119, 130–32, 148, 155–56
revenues: of higher education institutions,
  24–25, 35–36n43, 41n71; of online
  courses, 60, 61, 140. *See also* endowments; state governments
Rice, Andrew, 94n72
Robinson, Joan, 25
Rodriguez, Olga, 29n8

Rogers, Jenny, 30–31n17
Romanes Lecture, 44–45, 135, 139
Rosovsky, Henry, 138
Rothstein, Jesse, 39n64
Rouse, Cecilia, 39n64
Rudenstein, Neil L., 15, 33n29
Rudin, Robert S., 29nn9–11, 84n31

Sallie Mae/Ipsos survey, 20–21,
  36–37n50, 37n52
Sands, Tim, 94n72
San Jose State University, 117–18
Schneider, Eric C., 29nn9–11, 84n31
School of One, 94–95n73
Schumpeter, Joseph, 136
Seaman, Jeff, 90n55, 95n75
Seligson, Hannah, 95n80
Selingo, Jeff, 40–41nn70–71
Semester Online, 75
Sexton, John, 105
Shadish, William R., 83–84n29
Shahid, Abdus, 28n6
*The Shape of the River* (Bowen and Bok),
  23–24
shared governance, 64–66, 67. *See also*
  decision-making
Sherwin, Jay, 35n41
Shirky, Clay, 66–67, 92n63
Sloan Consortium, 72, 95n75
Smith, Joel, 80n14, 95n78
social media, 146
software. *See* online learning platforms
Solow, Robert, 6
Sparger, Elena, 94n72
sports, 13, 102, 127
SRI International, 78n9, 79n11
Stanford University: Class2Go platform,
  59, 86–87n40; dormitories of, 116;
  endowment of, 112–13; graduate programs of, 33n32; income sources of,
  113; Lyman presidency of, 69; medical
  school, 93n67, 113; MOOC spin-offs
  of, 74; reflection sessions of, 103; student aid at, 123; tuition and student
  aid trends at, 5, 110–13, 111f. *See also*
  Hennessy, John
state governments: higher education funding cuts by, 5, 19, 25, 36n44, 41n71,
  113, 114–15, 152; Medicaid spending